For Love and Money

Joyce White

Quality of Course

© 2000 QC Quality of Course Inc
38 McArthur Ave
Ottawa ON
K1L 6R2

QC Quality of Course Inc has used its best efforts in collecting and preparing material for inclusion in this book. It does not assume and hereby disclaims any liability to any party for any loss or damage caused by errors or omissions in the book, whether such errors or omissions result from negligence, accident or any other cause.

CANADIAN CATALOGUING IN PUBLICATION DATA
White, Joyce
For Love and Money: How to write romance novels
Includes index.
ISBN 1-895492-16-5
1. Love stories Authorship.   I. Title.
PN3377.5.R6W44 1994   808'.3'85   C94-900441-3

CONTENTS

CHAPTER ONE

SO, YOU WANT TO WRITE A ROMANCE

The love story is one of the oldest forms of literature, a part of every civilization since recorded history. The modern love story began with the fiction of writers such as Jane Austen and Margaret Mitchell, but it wasn't until the early 1960s that the category romance, as we know it today, became popular.

The first publisher to see a future for mass market romance was Harlequin's Richard Bonnycastle, who began buying rights from Mills & Boon Ltd., United Kingdom, in 1957. Fourteen years later, Harlequin bought out Mills & Boon, thereby gaining access to over 100 writers. The romance empire was founded.

The public's demand for romance fiction has been responsible for publishing companies aggressively seeking new writers. They offer large advances against royalties and multi-book contracts that a prolific writer can turn into an enviable income.

Not every good writer has what it takes to capture the essence of a love story. There is a special quality required to lift it past the boy-meets-girl formula of a few years ago. Increasing competition and public demand has forced editors to select only good quality manuscripts. The days of buying everything that came over the transom, are gone.

It is unlikely that you will find success unless you love romance. No how-to book can teach you to write the emotion necessary to touch your readers. That can only come from a romantic soul with a story to tell. But, you can learn to understand what makes these books work.

You can strengthen characterization, learn to develop realistic conflicts and satisfying resolutions. Dialogue will sparkle and narrative will be filled with descriptions that tease the senses. You can learn all the things that make romance fiction—romance.

If you are a lover of the genre, and have spent much of your spare time reading it, then you are halfway home. If not, start reading today. Pick up the books wherever you can: secondhand stores, garage sales, bazaars, book clubs. Ask friends to save them for you. Many are needed to give you an in-depth picture so you may as well collect them as economically as possible.

Read the first time for enjoyment. The second time, settle in with several coloured pens and start analyzing the book. Use separate colours for sexual tension, conflict, hooks, dialogue, tag words, heroine's description, hero's description, and so on. Highlight the sentences.

When you want to study the way a conflict begins and escalates into crisis, for example, all you have to do is read that colour. You will have a logical progression to the resolution and know if it is believable and satisfying.

Make notes in the flyleaf about what you like—and don't like. Write down those things you would change if you were writing the story. List your feelings about the protagonists and say why you fell in love with the hero or heroine. You did, didn't you?

Do this until you know you can write a romance; until the little voice inside your head is saying, I can do better than that. Don't be in a hurry to get started because the genre is here to stay.

The market is open. Anyone can break into the romance field. You don't need a name, a long publishing history or an agent, and the returns are excellent, even for a first book. Advances can be up to $10,000. Royalties follow at 6-10 percent of the cover price, and print runs are high.

Once you have learned the process of writing a romance, you can realistically pen a 50-55,000 word novel every month or two. You add it up. And you can learn to write a romance.

All you need is a measurable amount of creative talent, a love of the genre, the determination to succeed, and an understanding of what the editor wants. Many novelists make their debut this way, moving into mainstream fiction as their skills develop, and many established writers supplement their income by writing genre.

When you learn to write romance fiction, you learn skills that will improve all your writing. You create vivid word pictures, handle dialogue in a natural, relaxed way, and you develop plots that are exciting and fun to read.

As a writer of romance fiction, you are free to wander the globe, moving in circles you can only dream about, living in exotic lands through the characters you create. Research makes everything possible.

Of course, the more firsthand knowledge you have, the easier it will be. Initially, write about those places you know. Don't forget that your home is an exotic location to someone else. Many publishers produce books in several countries.

There is no age or sex discrimination. While romance fiction is called "women's fiction", and many writers are women, it is a discipline open to men. However, they usually write under a female pen name.

Who will ever forget England's Barbara Cartland, with hundreds of novels to her credit still writing long into her eighties? She is the perfect role model for any aspiring romance writer, with her flowing gowns, full makeup, sparkling jewels—and attitude.

Husband and wife teams have been successful, as have same-sex teams. One of the two may not feel comfortable with love scenes, while the other finds them fun to write. Another may have a strong dislike for writing dialogue, but can wring the last bit of emotion from any reader through superb narrative.

These teams work well, as long as there is no personality clash and the writing skills are at a comparable level. It takes special people to co-write a novel but, if you can do it, the rewards are many.

Your chance for financial success is good. Romance novels have a following, many selling to the same readers every month. These readers are loyal to favoured authors and they seek out the new releases. It doesn't take many books before you are looking at the difference between a secondhand compact and a new luxury car.

Your mainstream masterpiece may find a publisher but the odds of it making a large profit are slim. It takes years to build up a name that insures volume sales and to do that you need publishers willing to spend the dollars necessary to promote your work. Romance novels, by comparison, walk off the shelves with very little help from you or your publishing house.

Who are the romance readers? It was once believed that they were a small group of lonely women, living unbearable lives, who escaped into badly written fairy tales. I don't know if that were ever true, but it certainly isn't today. Understanding your reader can be the difference between success and failure.

Women and men read romances. Business people, professional people, homemakers; people from all backgrounds and with varied levels of education, read romances. There are novels for every age group and every interest.

Romance readers have one thing in common—they read to relax and have fun while they share the experiences you have created for them. The homemaker puts the kids down for a nap, pours a cup of coffee, and spends an hour on a Caribbean beach.

The businessman, with hours to kill during an international flight, takes his mind off the waiting pressures by losing himself in the arms of the sweet and sensitive heroine. The widow, or care-giver in a long relationship, recalls youthful times when love was filled with wonder.

I knew I wanted to write romance fiction the day I helped clear out an elderly relative's home after her death. Her marriage had been long and happy, but the last few years were spent caring for an invalid husband.

She never complained, never said she wished things were different. She was simply thankful that they were still together. After her husband died, she lived only a few months. When we started packing up her things, we discovered cupboards, bags, boxes—and boxes—of romance novels.

In each book she had written the date it was read, and reread, the reason she liked it, who she had lent it to—and their comments. This woman had a degree in English, a career in education, and a need to escape into a happier world than the one Fate had given her.

Romance fiction takes the reader to places where they can forget their troubles, where there is no violence and where, no matter how difficult the conflicts, the heroine and hero will resolve them to live happily ever after.

CHAPTER TWO

UNDERSTANDING ROMANCE CATEGORIES

You only need to look at the bookstore shelves to know there is a romance for every taste. They are filled with shiny covers that flaunt long-haired beauties locked in the arms of their muscle-bound heros, or women daintily racing across the moors, skirts billowing as they flee some threatening force that only the inside pages can reveal.

Confused? You have a right to be. It takes a considerable amount of time and much reading to understand the differences and similarities between the choices.

The word contemporary is liberally tossed about in publishers' guidelines, but what does it mean? Simply, contemporary romances are set in today's world. They have many degrees of sensuality and fit into many categories.

Historical romances are set in the past, against some period of history in Britain, Europe, or America. Erotic historicals were dubbed bodice rippers, a term that came from the hero's rough approach to the heroine's clothing.

There are categories within the categories: Sweet romance, erotic romance, Gothic, regency, historical, suspense, time travel, paranormal, and young adult romance. The only way to find out which one is for you is to read everything you think you might want to try.

Let's look at each line. Keep your interests and talent in mind as you go over them. You could get a starting point.

1. SWEET CATEGORY ROMANCE

Often called Traditional romance, this line is where most writers enter the field. They serve their apprenticeship, develop a distinctive style and then move on to the longer, more complicated titles.

Sweet romances are usually 50-60,000 words in length and have a simple plot. The emphasis is on the meeting of the protagonists, the growing relationship, and the conflicts that threaten to keep them apart.

Sexual attraction is strong and exciting to read, but physical contact is restricted to passionate embraces, breathless kisses, and yearning . . . lots of yearning. There is no explicit detail, even with today's openness where sex is concerned. These books are written for those people who prefer virginal heroines, and tender love that is left to the imagination of the reader.

However, this is romance so the ability to write sensually is essential. You need to appeal to all five senses through the vivid description of characters, places, food, clothing, surroundings. A dab of French perfume, the gold hoop attached to a delicate earlobe, the last bite of pastry fed to the heroine from the trembling hand of her love, helps to create a mood.

a) THE HEROINE is twenty to thirty years of age, often a little younger than the hero, and can be sexually inexperienced. If she is widowed, divorced, or has had a previous relationship, the sexual aspects are played down.

Our heroine holds traditional values but she is not old-fashioned. She is active in today's world whether she is a career woman, self-employed, or a full-time mother. She can be anything she chooses to be and she is ready to take on the hero. Usually, she falls in love with him because he is the only man who can beat her at her own game.

She is always portrayed with affection, has enough flaws so that the reader doesn't envy her and enough strengths so that the reader admires her. She does the things every woman wants to do.

At the end of the book, the heroine "grows" and becomes a better person from her association with the hero.

b) THE HERO is usually in his mid-twenties to late thirties. He is attractive, worldly, and successful by his own definition. He does not have to be a millionaire but he must succeed in his chosen field.

The author's job is to make every woman reading the book fall in love with the hero. She must sigh when the heroine sighs, experience each heartbreak and disappointment, and shed a tear when the hero finally sweeps his lady-love into his arms. If you, the creator of the hero, don't fall in love with him neither will your reader.

Today's hero is completely rounded, with truly heroic qualities. There is a balance between strength and gentleness. He is no longer a "love them and leave them" kind of guy, or a throwback to the dashing rake. His strengths and vulnerabilities complement the heroine's strengths and vulnerabilities.

Readers want men who are independent, who have the sensitivity to reveal their imperfections and can display a natural authority without emotional abuse. They must be willing to commit—to a cause, a family, a community and, eventually, to the heroine.

The hero is confident and sure of himself without the need to prove it all the time. He won't stand still for unfairness but he will turn the other cheek where the heroine is concerned. If he is wealthy, he doesn't flaunt his money, and he is never, never, a "sugar daddy."

Glamour and glitz are still popular but the hero is not the polished, silent-bordering-on-cruel, man of a few years ago. He is a "rough gem", waiting for the woman who can bring out all the facets of his personality.

Men today can be single fathers but not in the same sense as the Gothic, with their Lord of the Manor and Nanny storylines. These fathers go to parent-teacher meetings, they cook and clean, and can do everything the woman can do . . . and they face the same problems with the children. They do not give the kids to the Nanny and vanish to places unknown, surfacing only when it's time to make the heroine's heart pound.

Pay close attention to the hero in the books you read because his importance is often overlooked. Writing an out-of-date hero will likely get you a rejection. Keep one thing in mind—this is a nice guy who is every father's nightmare!

c) THE PLOT of the sweet romance has just enough complexity to maintain interest. Subplots (mystery, suspense, adventure) can be used as long as they don't take away from the love story.

The stories are traditional, with that fresh, individual approach only you can supply. Always strive for the one element that will catch an editor's attention.

Conflicts result from the actions and reactions of the protagonists. The word length limits you, so be sure the complication is logical, complex enough to be sustainable, and one that can be resolved in a believable way.

The resolution is the high point of your story. It is here that the protagonists declare their undying love. Don't cheat your readers. If you can put the two of them in a room and let them talk out their differences, then you have missed the mark. (Conflict and resolution is detailed in a further chapter.)

The plot is not grounded in harsh realities. While everything must be plausible, this is escapist fiction—the fulfillment of dreams.

d) SEX scenes are tempered. There is no explicit description and the protagonists do not sleep together before marriage, although they would like to. They indulge in passionate kisses, resist temptation, and dream about the day they will be together. The emphasis is always on the emotional, never on the physical.

e) THE SETTING can be anywhere in the world but, wherever you place it, be sure you know what you're talking about. Initially, it is best to stay with those locations you know well—your hometown, for example. Later, when you are comfortable with the format, you can write from research.

One of the biggest mistakes that new writers make is letting the background intrude on the romance. You are not writing a travelogue. Everything in the setting must add to the feeling and be integrated in a way that heightens the senses.

f) STYLE is light, natural and often humorous. A word of caution: Humour should not be attempted if you do not have the natural ability to write it, or if it doesn't fit the story. You are aiming for a clear, individual style that is not pretentious; one that is original and not merely an imitation of another writer.

The dialogue should reflect the way people speak, without overusing dialect or idiom. Profanity and sensual comment should be kept at a minimum, if used at all.

2. SENSUAL CATEGORY ROMANCE

These intense, dramatic stories, often set in exotic locations, are the best-selling romance line in the world. They are 50-60,000 words in length, and are characterized by explicit descriptions of lovemaking between the protagonists. No restrictions are placed on the author's imagination.

Writing sex scenes can be difficult for the new writer, or for one who feels inhibited. If you are uncomfortable with, his tongue invaded the deep, warm recesses of her mouth, or taut, tingling nipples, then this is not the line for you.

These romances reflect today's world, the ever-changing social and economic scene. It is important to keep up with the shifts in thinking that set the standards for relationships between men and women. Television and radio talk shows, newspapers, and magazines should become part of your life.

Subjects that were taboo yesterday provide fresh situations for romance novels today. Almost anything goes, as long as it is handled in the context of the romance and is presented in good taste. The still unacceptable topics include violence, particularly against women, rape, and gratuitous sex scenes.

a) THE HEROINE stands on the brink of tomorrow's world. She is the personification of the contemporary woman: strong-willed, determined, interesting and intelligent. She is also very attractive.

Her age and career depend on the plot. She can be a twenty-year old experiencing the professional world for the first time, or she can be a seasoned lawyer taking on the cases no one else wants. If your story calls for a single mother, struggling to meet the demands of daily life, that's fine, too.

What she can never be is promiscuous. She can be sexually experienced, but only when she has always been in love and part of a meaningful relationship. She evolves as a character during the course of the story and becomes a better person from being with the hero.

b) THE HERO is often older than the heroine and usually more experienced. He is a real presence in the story, charismatic and powerful. He is attractive and confident, with an aura of sexuality, but he is not arrogant—although he may give that impression in the beginning of the book.

Whatever the profession he chooses, he is successful. The days of the mandatory doctor, lawyer, high-roller, are gone. Today, our hero can be a school teacher, struggling to make ends meet, but he is the best school teacher the district has ever seen.

A successful sensual romance places more emphasis on the hero. Scenes are written from his point of view as well as from the heroine's. His thoughts, dreams and desires are made known, and his vulnerability is endearing. The reader will fall in love with him as deeply as the heroine does.

c) THE PLOT is more complex than the sweet romance. There is room to develop secondary characters who are usually cast to provide added conflict. Sub-plots may be used if they don't detract from the romance.

The emphasis is on a love so intense that it is a once-in-a-lifetime happening, changing the protagonists forever. Any situation may be used that is part of life today, providing it is kept within the limits of good taste. There is no violence, racial slurs, homosexuality or drug use by the protagonists.

Convincing characters, coping with genuine obstacles that are not removed until the final pages of the book, are part of this line's appeal. There must be enough realistic conflict to keep them apart and maintain the sexual tension. If the protagonists meet and they are immediately compatible, the story loses its excitement.

d) SEX plays a greater part in the sensual romance than in the sweet romance. There is a high degree of sexual tension, sensuality, and more explicitly written scenes, but the emphasis is still on emotion. Clinical detail is avoided.

The degree of sexual description depends on what is appropriate for the protagonists and the situation. While the conflict demands that the characters are not instantly compatible, there is instant sexual attraction. Explosive energy runs like a high-voltage wire between them.

e) THE SETTING can be anywhere in the world but it must be romantic. The readers of sensual romance are seeking emotional escape through their journeys to interesting and colourful places that are important to the mood of the story.

When you write a sensual romance, you need the ability to vividly convey your background. The sights and sounds of the streets, the walks through flower gardens or along beaches, the colours and the scents and the feelings, are written within the context of the story.

Again, you are not writing a travelogue. What you are doing is transporting the reader to a desired place where everything is experienced: scenery, people, food, clothing, climate—everything!

Traditional roles and lifestyles have given way to new ones. Women are no longer bound by the conventions of society and that is exciting for romance writers.

f) THE STYLE should show the intensity of falling in love. You are not faced with the limitations of the sweet romance novel but you still need to write in a clear, natural style that carries an element of excitement. The writing should never be mediocre but nor should it be so dramatic that it becomes absurd.

3. SENSUOUS ROMANCE

This line of romance runs between 60-100,000 words, depending on the publishing house. The length gives you scope to develop characters and subplots and the format lets your imagination run wild.

Bold, sometimes controversial, these stories focus on contemporary relationships between adults, and are pure romantic fantasy.

a) THE HEROINE is an attractive North American woman, single, divorced or married. She is no younger than 23 years and her age should be in keeping with the context of the story.

This is a very up-to-date woman. She juggles a career she is passionate about with the trials of her personal life, and she does it well because she has a strong sense of her own identity.

Our heroine has one desire in life that surpasses all others—she wants to find the man who can fulfill her emotionally and sexually, and is willing to make a lifetime commitment.

b) THE HERO is comparable in age to the heroine, may or may not be North American, and is about as sexy as a man can be. He is handsome, self-assured, and successful at his job and everything else he tries. A forceful, charismatic, larger-than-life kind of guy who plays an active part in the story.

Writing this character can be fun because the options are many. He can be anything from a "rough-edged" bad boy to the sensitive, humorous man of the Nineties. But, whichever he is, his life is forever changed by his love for the heroine.

The hero is immediately attracted to the heroine and soon finds that attraction to be all-consuming. He might fight against his desire for her but she is always on his mind.

Both points of view are used in these books. The reader is privy to the hero's thoughts and dreams, understands his motivations, and sees his vulnerabilities. Above all, the reader falls in love.

c) THE PLOT focuses on the developing romance with any subplots included only to enrich it. It must be original, with a fresh approach to characterization, action-oriented, and complex enough to sustain the word count.

Good dialogue is essential as there is minimal use of narrative, but dialect and jargon should be avoided. Narrative passages act as transitions for the action, and to enhance the sensual experience.

Strong, believable conflicts are essential to this line and they cover a wide range of subjects: sexual and emotional fantasy, topical and controversial themes, glitz and glamour, adventure. They are innovative stories that push the boundaries.

d) SEX is bold and sensuous, with a high degree of sexual tension necessary to maintain the feelings of arousal.

The protagonists have many sensual encounters and they consummate their relationship at an appropriate point in the story.

Love scenes are highly erotic, emotional, and realistic but, above all, they are fun. The author must be comfortable with this format or the encounters will not be believed.

e) THE SETTING can be anywhere in the world but the stories are written from a North American point of view. It is important that the author has a feel for the location, and to write in such a way that it becomes a backdrop for the romance.

Attention should be paid to details. They should add to the sensory aspect of the story and heighten the pleasure.

f) THE STYLE is similar to the softer lines but the author has more latitude. Language can be stronger, descriptions detailed, and themes more complex. There are no restrictions placed on the author's imagination.

4. REGENCY ROMANCE

The author needs to understand England's Regency period (1811-1820) because these books are 50-75,000 words of detail about dress, food, housing, speech and customs. They must be accurate. Research is essential.

Keep research notes on index cards or in a file. Pictures are valuable and should be clipped and saved in folders under headings of dress, hairstyles, furnishings, and so on. Be sure to date everything you collect so when you are looking for material dealing with a specific time, it will be easily found.

Read and take notes if you come across something that could be useful, if not for your current work, then for something in the future. Reading Regency Romances is the best way to learn about and to understand the genre.

The Regency period was a special time in England's history. Elegant architecture, terraces, huge green spaces and gardens surrounding lofty mansions added to the charm. Fashion was changing rapidly and girls were cutting their hair.

The appeal of the period lies in the fact that it is far enough removed from the present to be romantic but not so far as to be uncivilised. People's selection of food and dress, their social customs, and manners, was not too distant from our own. The differences, such as the lack of telephones and the modes of transportation, add to the interest without being foreign.

Another attraction is that Recency romances are written about the aristocracy. What better trappings for a romance than wealth and power, satin and lace, fine wines and beautiful people? The trick to these romances is to find that irresistible blend of fiction and fact that makes the period come alive for the reader without giving him an indigestible amount of detail.

a) THE HEROINE is exotically beautiful, full-bosom with a slender waist and well-turned ankles.

Her hair is long and lustrous, beckoning the hero to bury his face, in the fragrant, silky strands.

She is usually 18-25 years of age and from an aristocratic family. If fate has deemed her to be poor, her background is always respectable. No matter what her standing, she is well versed in the social graces, has a quick wit and a playful manner, and a strong incentive to get married.

b) THE HERO is between 25 and 36 years old. He is exceedingly well educated for the time; elegant and erudite, dashing and virile. His time is occupied with an important business or political concern, but he has been known to indulge in gambling, horse racing, duelling and drinking—the amusements of society.

Our hero is pursued by the mother of every eligible female for miles around. He is the catch of the season. For reasons unbeknownst to the heroine, he has never been married. Often this is the setting for the story's conflict.

c) THE PLOT is generally light and lively. The theme is usually simple: a rather impoverished, though well-born, heroine falls in love with, and in the end marries, the rich hero. Occasionally, the heroine is wealthy in her own right and then the problem becomes weeding out fortune hunters.

Adventure is a large part of the Regency romance. Highwaymen and smugglers, espionage and intrigue, are only some of the things with which our heroine has to contend.

Social comedy is another favourite ploy. The accidental or impulsive deception that leads the hero or heroine to believe one or the other is not what they seem. Usually, this has to do with a pretence of wealth or position, and it can lead to humorous consequences that add to the conflict between the protagonists.

There can be one or more subplots involving secondary characters as long as they are kept in the background. Nothing must overshadow the romance.

The heroine's point of view dominates although the hero's point of view can be used, in moderation, as the storyline requires it to move the plot.

The Recency should be a fun, romantic romp. Controversial themes, or subplots involving crime, corruption, and poverty, are not suitable for this line.

d) SEX is kept to a minimum and is never graphically described. It is understood that offstage the gentlemen have their dalliances, and that the heroine wisely turns a blind eye, but the actions are never presented to the reader.

The scenes that reveal the protagonist's affection and attraction for each other are in keeping with their social position. Chemistry is essential if you are going to sustain a level of sexual tension.

e) THE SETTING in Regency romance is more defined than in any of the other lines. You are confined to a ten year period when fashion was changing rapidly and women were dampening their petticoats to make them cling to their bodies.

The novel must be filled with details: blue velvet drapery in the sitting room, beige silk shoes on the heroine's dainty feet, lush gardens and exquisite food. You need the skill to make your readers believe they are a part of the time.

f) THE STYLE is in keeping with the period. Attention must be paid to dialogue. It is too easy to slip in modern usage and shatter the atmosphere you've so carefully created. You may find a copy of Samuel Johnson's Dictionary helpful to give you the correct English usage.

You do not always have to use period speech if the characters and setting are convincing. Plain, formal speech, without slang, and with a smattering of fashionable expression, is sufficient to create a regency atmosphere.

5. HISTORICAL ROMANCE

These are brash, bold, action-packed stories that take place some time in the past. American Historical romances capture the spirit of America. Erotic Historical romances are intensely sensual and graphic. Period Historical romances are true to the culture and events of the time in which they are set and let the reader experience history through the lives of fascinating characters. The story should focus on the heroine and how her love for one man changes her life.

Plots are set between 1600 and 1900, although a really good story set in an earlier time may be considered by some publishers. They are 70-105,000 words in length, depending on the publishing house.

When you write historical novels, you can build on the romantic feelings many people have for the past.

The research must be thorough. You want your readers to learn something new about the period while losing themselves in the world you have created.

a) THE HEROINE, eighteen to twenty-four years of age, is strong and sassy, attractive, and has the confidence to tackle anything that comes her way, including the hero.

The chosen period is your guide for her actions. Obviously, the 1890 American woman is not going to behave in the same way as the 1700's woman living in London, England. Study the customs of the day and then write your heroine larger than life.

Her personality is aggressive for the time. She is stubborn and strong-willed, often difficult, but she softens whenever the hero is around. She is also emotionally vulnerable. Although the historical period has placed her in circumstances that may be unfamiliar to the reader, she reacts in a familiar way; therefore, becoming a sympathetic character.

b) THE HERO is usually older than the heroine. He is bold and brash, rugged around the edges, earthy, and is the sexiest man in the world. There is not a shred of doubt in the reader's mind as to his sexual prowess.

He takes charge of everything, even when he is met with opposition. He has a lust for adventure, a hunger for challenge and a thirst for daring. The reader envisions a savagely aggressive male animal, with taut muscles and eyes that pierce like swords, and longs to tame him—the same emotions that he arouses in the heroine.

As with the heroine, the hero's actions and reactions will depend on the period. The frontiersman will have the rugged edges and lust for adventure that the seventeenth century male has, but he may not have the arrogant belief that all women are trollops at heart.

In historical romance the hero can be the central character (hero-led) or have a shared point of view with the heroine. There is more room to develop his character, to see him grow as a person, and to watch him fall in love. The one thing to keep in mind is that this guy is not the boy next door.

c) THE PLOT is fast-paced, action-filled and upbeat. These books are written with tongue in cheek and a great deal of humour—if you can write humour naturally. They are period fairy tales in which the characters conquer all to win every heart's desire.

The stories aim for fictional credibility, not realism, but it is vital that the events and culture of the period be well-developed and authentic. You need in-depth research.

You must have a good knowledge of the dress, custom, food, living habits, medicine, education, transportation, communication, and speech patterns of the day. If you don't know, don't guess. Somewhere, there is a history buff who is more than willing to check up on you if you make a mistake. Too many errors and you lose your credibility—and your audience.

The unfolding romance is the focus of the story. Since you are free to use both points of view, you have more freedom to develop the plot and the characters.

There is room for secondary characters and subplots. Sometimes they are necessary to solve problems you discover as you write. For example, the back-lacing of corsets requires the heroine to have a maid. Give her a unique personality and she can grow into a major secondary character.

These plots are often filled with twists and turns, making the addition of secondary characters necessary. They are used as sounding-boards for the protagonists' shared thoughts and secrets, to move the action, and to explain motivation.

It is the interaction between all the characters that makes the plot exciting—a story that the reader will long remember after the last page is turned.

d) SEX ranges from intensely passionate to erotic, depending on the category you are writing. The publisher's guidelines give you the exact level each requires. One thing every line has in common is they are filled with sexual tension and all the emotions of falling in love.

e) THE SETTING grounds each of these novels in the ambience of the particular time in which they are placed. Obviously, a story set in some frontier settlement is not going to have the same elements as a story set in a British Court.

The sense of place is important but it should not take precedence over the romance. Details should enrich the experience and make the past truly come alive.

f) THE STYLE is probably more important in these novels than in any of the other lines. The writer must be forever diligent, never "stepping out of character" through the use of inappropriate dialogue or bogus detail.

To write historical romances you have to read them. Lots of them. They have a rhythm all their own. They are created by magicians who take you to a place in the past where you can share the food, wear the clothes, and live in the homes.

The reader should be able to smell the herbs gently tucked into the heroine's ivory satin pillow and sense her longing as she dreams about the hero. No detail is too small, no turn of phrase too quaint, if it depicts the period and brings the characters to life. The style of your writing colours the picture you have drawn.

6. ROMANTIC SUSPENSE

These books blend mystery, suspense and adventure with the excitement of romance. The focus of the plot is now on the mystery/suspense element that was relegated to a subplot in the other lines. The count runs 70-100,000 words.

Romantic suspense has been described as contemporary Gothic novels, or women-in-jeopardy. An appealing heroine, living alone, is threatened by some ominous force. Only her courage, presence of mind, and the hero can save her from her plight.

Subject matter ranges from murder mysteries, psychological suspense, adventure and thrillers, to everyday occurrences with a twist. It gives you more options than most forms of the genre. There is constant interaction between the protagonists who, by working together, solve the puzzle or the problem while falling in love. As with any romance, the resolution is satisfying and the story ends happily.

a) THE HEROINE is usually a young girl in the Gothic novel, a mature woman in the mystery and, as the storyline dictates, everywhere in between. The one thing she always is, is active in solving the puzzle.

Our heroine contributes her knowledge and skill to work side by side with the hero. He could not solve the mystery without her. She has courage but shows vulnerability, takes risks but usually with support from the hero, and she is fiercely loyal.

Her physical appearance will depend on the line you are writing. Gothic heroines usually have flowing hair and rustling gowns, while the modern heroine can have cropped hair and blue jeans. The writer's job is to make her fit the story.

b) THE HERO is a mature man, older than the heroine in the Gothic and of comparable age in the contemporary novels.

The hero of the contemporary romance is an attractive man in both personality and physical appearance. He complements the heroine in knowledge and skill, so that together they may solve the problem. He is sensitive and caring, but never weak; strong-willed but never abusive; sexy to the point of being dangerous.

The hero in a Gothic novel is often the silent type, sometimes taken for the villain, but he is really a sensitive guy who is misunderstood. He usually harbours a deep secret that can become the focal point of the mystery.

The hero and heroine do not have to be on the same side. They can be working against each other (the lawyer and the District Attorney, for example) but at some point in the story they come together and realize they have a common goal . . . and that they are falling in love.

c) THE PLOT for the Gothic novel is more "formula fiction" than are the other types of romantic suspense. The Gothic novel displays the had I but known characteristic . . . Had I but known there was a body in the bell tower; an evil twin brother; quicksand in the bog.

The heroine is often in a position of servitude, a Nanny, for instance, and is living in a place that frightens her. But, she doesn't want to leave because she has fallen in love with the moody, brooding, and emotionally crippled hero, or she cannot leave because she is physically isolated, an island for example.

Usually, she feels a sense of responsibility for another character, her young ward, or some other dependent creature. While mysterious and frightening events unfold around her, it becomes clear that her survival, and her sanity, depend on her solving the mystery.

Sometimes, she doesn't realize, until it's too late, that she is being threatened. The problem with this is, if the threat is so vague that the heroine doesn't see it, the reader will likely miss it also.

She may lose her courage and run off in panic, she may be too shy or frightened to fight the threat, or she may go for help but fail to convince anyone that she is in danger. in Gothic novels, it is always the hero who comes to her rescue and that usually happens in the last few pages of the book.

The secret of these books is: the heroine must be in danger and confront that danger, but the meat of the story is why she confronts the danger.

In contemporary romantic suspense, the protagonists meet on an equal footing in an action-oriented, complex and realistic plot with enough twists to avoid a predictable ending. The dilemma presents itself early in the book and must be complex enough to sustain the storyline for at least 70,000 words.

The romantic relationship grows and develops with the plot as the shared dangers bring the protagonists closer together. The heroine can be responsible for "saving" the hero or they can take turns "saving" each other but it is the sharing of danger that leads to the sharing of passions.

All clues must be tied up by the end of the book.

d) SEX does not detract from the tension and pacing of the plot. Love scenes are acceptable but they must come about as a direct result of an action or interaction dictated by the plot, and they must fit naturally into the story.

Sexual tension, resulting from shared dangers and the protagonists close proximity to each other, is essential to show the developing romance. This is romance, not mystery. You cannot write a "who-done-it" and throw in a kiss.

e) THE SETTING can be anywhere in the world providing it is presented accurately. If you are going to centre your mystery in New Orleans during Mardi Gras, or in the Caribbean battling a hurricane, it helps if you have been there. If you are relying on research, you must be thorough.

The main purpose of the setting is to enhance the suspense. Location can add atmosphere and excitement, and give the reader a feeling of being part of the mystery. It becomes fun when danger is experienced from a safe distance.

f) THE STYLE is in keeping with the action. The Gothic has a different tone than the New York detective romp, and neither one sounds like Romancing the Stone. Dialogue should contain just enough of the vernacular to give the story authenticity, and to let the reader distinguish between speakers. It is fast-paced and mimics the way people talk.

Narrative is rich with description, whether you are writing Gothic or contemporary novels. The reader experiences the heroine's terror as she runs barefoot through the castle's darkened halls, or the hero's struggle to find the New York mugger before the heroine does.

Readers often follow an author because they like the distinctive style. It is important to develop your own voice, and you do that by writing. The more you practise, the stronger your style becomes.

7. NEW DIRECTIONS IN ROMANCE

A whole new category of romance has been invading the market. These are the romances that have a fantasy element. They include time-travel and futuristic plotlines. The reader's imagination takes the story to places unheard of in the genre, only a short time ago.

This is a popular series, growing as readers and authors discover the benefits of stories set in lavish lands on distant worlds. The subject matter, and the detail necessary to make these novels believable, leads to books that are 100-115,000 words in length.

Examples of subjects that have worked are: Historical romances that include time travel, Futuristic romances that propel the heroine into another world in our time (an alternate existence), into space, or onto another planet. Ghost romances have also proven to be popular.

Futuristic romance should not depend on science fiction hardware or technology. You are aiming for a world that is not unlike the world we know today. The people and customs are familiar but the lifestyle is projected.

Time-travel goes a step further. A modern day heroine or hero goes back in time and falls in love with someone from that era. They are usually sensual romances with strong plots and carefully thought out characters.

The challenge is to maintain credibility during the transition between past and present without the use of a time machine. The characters pass through a "space portal", experience some molecular metamorphosis, or live through some natural phenomenon that places them in another time. Conflicts and resolutions arise from the protagonists belonging to different eras.

The characters can travel back, letting the reader view history through the eyes of someone from our time, or they can travel forward and experience a world that might be. There is no philosophizing about fate, the meaning of time, or how the past will affect the future.

These books can be as much fun to write as they are to read. If you think you want to try this line after you've read several books and studied the guidelines, a good place to start is with a familiar historical incident.

For example, go back to the time of Napoleon and be Josephine's handmaiden. Fall in love with one of the men off to the Battle of Waterloo . . . and then see where the story takes you.

8. YOUNG ADULT ROMANCE

These are very sweet romances written for teens. They are about 40,000 words in length and have simple plots that deal with contemporary problems. Today, that can be adoption, drugs, peer pressure, and emotional conflicts.

The heroine is usually a year or two older than your target audience. She has a crush on a boy her own age and experiences the first pangs of love. The emotional attraction is intense but the physical attraction is kept to hand holding and a stolen kiss.

Having the protagonists involved in an adventure helps keep these books action-oriented. You must read several, aimed at the different age levels, if you are to be successful in this line. Teens have a language all their own, and it is constantly changing.

There are other romance lines but these are the major categories, the ones that seem to stay year after year. Maybe you have a good idea which one you want to write. Perhaps you are still unsure.

The following chapters will take you through characterization, dialogue, outlines and plot structure, sexual tension, conflicts and resolution. They should help you decide where you want to be.

The true test of writing comes from reading. You will find yourself enjoying one or two of the lines more than you do the others, and that's where you should begin.

Writers successful in the field have read hundreds of romance novels and you must, too.

CHAPTER THREE

YOUR ROMANTIC LIFE

You have read books from every line and marked them with coloured pens. You have selected a category, written pages of notes, and now you can't wait to get started.

Setting up your work space is one of the most important things you will do before you begin to write. Everything around you must cultivate a feeling of romance. It doesn't matter whether you are in a large, sunlit room of your own, or stuck in a corner of the kitchen, that space has to envelop you.

Cover the walls with pictures of romantic places, photographs of beautiful people, even the covers from your favourite books. Keep a single rose in a crystal vase. Surround yourself with the colours that make you happy and play soft music in the background.

There is nothing romantic about clutter so get organized right from the start. You need a simple filing system that can expand to meet the demands of a growing career. A small cabinet, or a cardboard box large enough to hold file folders, should be your starting point.

Label the folders with those things you are using: editorial correspondence, guidelines, work in progress, tear sheets (copies of published work), and so on. As your needs change, modify the labels. Eventually, you will have one folder for each publisher that will hold incoming and outgoing correspondence and tip sheets. Others will contain reference material, copies of manuscripts, accounts receivable and payable, and anything else you find necessary.

A backup should be kept on file cards. They give you instant access to manuscript submission information, editorial changes, publishing dates, and completed sales. This file may also be kept on the computer but that should not be the only storage system. Computers do fail and material can be lost. There is also the inconvenience of exiting a programme if you need to access file information. The equipment you buy should be the best you can afford. A computer is no longer a luxury. It is a necessity. Many publishers are requesting work be submitted on disk and hard copy. Don't lose sight of why you need a computer and, unless you have money to play with, buy only those programmes that relate to your work.

A good word processing package, with an extra programme for editing, and the capacity for expansion, is all you require. Later, if you find you have use for additional programmes, you can add to your system.

A fax machine is another piece of equipment that has moved out of the luxury class. It saves vast amounts of money and time, and seems to demand a more immediate response. Submission by fax is outlined in the publisher's editorial guidelines. They are all different so be sure to check before you send your work.

Computer generated faxes are improving. The advantage is that you can send directly from your computer to your editor's fax machine by fax modem, or to his computer by modem. Entire manuscripts can be electronically transferred if the editor accepts material in that format.

Don't get rid of your typewriter. Envelopes and shipping labels are easier to type than they are to print on a computer. Also, if your system goes down, you can continue to work on drafts, if not on finished copy.

A good printer, bookshelves, a comfortable chair, a desk other than the computer desk if you have room, and a place to keep paper, disks, card files, etc., make up the rest of the office.

How you turn it into a romantic space is up to you. A writer friend of mine dresses Barbie and Ken dolls in her characters' costumes and places them around the room. Another has pictures of her family and another, her favorite screen stars. Do the things that work for you.

Your next step is to set up research files. You can use some space in your cabinet or keep them separate. These files include general information and data collected for your current work.

Again, the system will grow with your needs. Initially, label folders: Hero, heroine, secondary characters, clothing, food, accommodation, gardens, exotic locations, and careers. These can be subdivided as required.

Your general file will contain all the clippings from newspapers and magazines, notes, maps, travel folders, menus, etc., that you think could be useful in the future.

The work-in-progress file holds all the information that has to do with the protagonists, setting, background, career, etc. As you finish with the material, move it back into the general file.

Card files work well for keeping track of details. They give you quick reference to things like room decor, the heroine's favourite restaurant, a character's eye and hair colour. You would be amazed how often a blue-eyed hero has flashing dark eyes in the middle of a book.

You're all set. You are happy in your romantic, well-organized environment, and you have a wonderful idea just begging to be written. Don't be in a hurry. Take the time to follow these suggestions and you'll save yourself hours of rewriting.

Buy a large, three-ring binder, lined paper and a couple of packages of dividers. Label the dividers: hero, heroine, secondary characters (you may want one section for each, depending on the length of the book), setting, major conflicts, plot, subplot with secondary conflicts, resolutions, and chapter outline.

At the back of the binder, keep a section for vocabulary and another for story ideas. If you find a word or phrase you like, or write something you may want to use again, enter it in the vocabulary list. Jot down story ideas as they come to you, and keep a list of names and titles.

Start with the heroine: Age, eye and hair colour, height and weight, physical characteristics, strengths and weaknesses. Write about her childhood, teen years, educational background, association with family members, career, love interests, friends, preferences in food, clothing and living style, dreams, desires and disappointments.

Write a paragraph about her background. Where was she born? Under which astrological sign? How many brothers and sisters does she have? Their names? Are her parents still alive? Write about them. What influences in her background have given her the strengths (self-assurance, bravery, etc.) and weaknesses (impatience, temperament, etc.) that affect her life.

In short, you want to know everything there is to know. You won't use all this data, but you must know it to write a well-rounded and believable character. When the background work is completed, move on to the interview.

You really are going to interview your heroine and she is going to answer you in first-person. Let the questions and answers flow. Write down the first things that come into your head and soon your character will take on a personality of her own. Some answers will surprise you. The following list will help you to get started.

1. What are you keeping secret?
2. How well do you know/like yourself?
3. What are you lying about—if only to yourself?
4. What do you like/admire about yourself?

5. A friend described your personality. How was he/she right? Wrong? Why?
6. In what situation is your self-esteem most at risk?
7. In what situation are you frightened?
8. In what situation are you brave?
9. How well do your friends know you?
10. What does your lover know about you that no one else knows? What kind of power does this love give you?
11. How has your life affected your personality?
12. What do you want from life?
13. What do you need to overcome?
14. What, in the outside world, is preventing you from completing these goals?
15. What, in yourself, is preventing you?
16. What must happen to enable you to overcome this?
17. In relationships, how are you different with family than with friends. Why?
18. Is there anyone in your life that you are attracted to? Tell me about him?
19. What scares you about this man?
20. What do you think he can do for you that no one else can?
21. What is your initial perception of a stranger?
22. Do you try to charm, or to deceive, people when you first meet them?
23. How are you with rivals?
24. When you first walk into a room, what do you notice? The people, the furniture, etc.?
25. Are you really sensual?
26. How do you see the world?

27. How do you best learn? Trial and error?

28. How do you decide if you can trust someone?

29. How do you fall in love? Suddenly? Slowly?

30. What parts of loving come easy to you? Hard?

31. What is your goal in life?

32. Describe yourself to me.

Do this for every character in the book, no matter how minor his or her role. It is wise to do only one a day. If you try to do the hero and the heroine simultaneously, you are going to have an overlap of personality.

As you work with the interview, questions other than those you have prepared will arise. Ask them. This is a fun part of the writing process but it does take time. Don't try to rush it. The more attention you pay to detail when you are setting up the novel, the easier it will be to write.

Once your characters are in place, and you have extensive notes in the binder and quick reference notes on cards, go on to planning the setting. This is the where the romance happens so everything about it has to be romantic.

Your heroine walks in the moonlight, along fragrant, petal-lined paths. Your hero slams the door and sinks into the butter-soft leather chair, behind his polished-oak desk. Everything they do, and everywhere they go, interests your reader.

Unless you are writing a historical romance, it is wise to start with your own city, or one you know well. Beautiful places and excellent restaurants that are ordinary to you, are exotic to someone else.

This is where your file comes in handy. You have collected Chamber of Commerce brochures, newspaper clippings, maps, restaurant menus, pictures of houses and gardens—everything it takes to make a life. Now you put them to use.

In your binder, describe in detail the city where your characters live, the streets they live on and the houses they live in. Write about the buildings and the decor of the rooms. Remember, this is romance. You want to include everything that adds to the aura: The scent of spring flowers filling the foyer; the soft lapping of waves against the sun-bathed beach; the summer breeze drifting through an open window to bathe the lovers in warmth.

Pay attention to period architecture and furnishings. If your story is set in a specific era, study magazines and library reference material so that your 17th century heroine doesn't end up living in a highrise apartment. Know the style of the chairs, the type of upholstery and the colour preferences. Don't guess.

The same rule applies for clothing, food, china, etc. Readers want to know everything about the characters—what they are wearing, where they live and work, what they ate for dinner. Dining out is a favourite pastime of romance characters. Your audience really does want to know what was on the menu when the hero took the heroine's hand and gazed into her eyes.

If they are dining seaside in the Virgin Islands, get yourself a Caribbean cookbook. At Mardi Gras? Make sure you know Cajun cuisine. It helps if you have tasted what the heroine is enjoying, so start cooking if you can't eat out.

By now, you know your characters inside and out. You know where and how they live, and the part they'll play in your story. It's time to give them some problems.

In the section labelled conflicts, list the difficulties facing your lovers. You need to examine internal and external conflicts and, the most important conflict, sexual tension between the hero and heroine.

For sexual tension to escalate to a titillating level, you must conceive, and then emphasize, convincing reasons for the lovers to misunderstand each other while you fan the flame of the attraction between them.

Put huge obstacles in their paths, not little hurdles. It must seem to the protagonists that they will never resolve their problems—that love will not conquer all! To the readers, this is a tragedy because they know how much in love the protagonists really are. Developing complications and conflicts is detailed later in the book.

Internal conflicts are those that generate from within the characters. The heroine may have loved and lost. Now she is afraid to trust men. The hero may have had a domineering mother. Now he is afraid of strong women. These conflicts are the emotional problems that come between the characters and their romance.

External conflicts are the problems that are outside the characters' control. They are the physical things that keep them apart: family influence, differences of opinion, career conflicts, and events in the story.

Both internal and external conflicts are necessary to balance and sustain the romance. Too many emotional problems and you are faced with weak, even whiny, characters. Too many external conflicts and you run the risk of having a reader shake his head in disbelief.

For each conflict there must be a resolution. The minor complications are solved as the plot unfolds. They are the peaks and valleys of the story. The major conflict that threatens to separate the lovers forever is not resolved until the last pages of the book.

Conflict and resolution must be worked out before you start. If you set out to write your story without knowing what each problem is and how it will resolve, you may forget to tie up loose ends or you may finish everything too quickly.

You might find it easier to work out conflicts and resolutions together instead of separately. A later chapter is devoted to building strong conflicts and satisfying resolutions.

Now you are ready to get to the heart of your novel. Under plot, write a few pages about your story, covering both plot and theme. Plot is the story itself, theme is the point you want to make. For example, you are writing about the adventures of two people on a cruise: The plot. They are falling in love: The theme.

This section is used as a pre-outline. It helps to organize your thoughts and to put them in the chronological order that will become the chapters. Contradictions in logic will show up as your characters start to live.

Subplots should be included only if they add to the story. They should move the main action to the conclusion or they should serve to enhance a major characters' development. If they are thrown in because you think it would be fun to write about a car chase, for example, they won't work.

The same holds true for secondary characters. While you do need to do a complete workup and interview so that you will understand them, they must be included for a reason. They can be used as a sounding board for the protagonists' thoughts, a vehicle to bring the lovers together or tear them apart, and as a means of transition.

When the plot and theme are clear in your mind, begin your section on chapter outlines. This is an important part of the structure, but what you do is not written in stone. Don't feel intimidated simply because you've put some words on paper.

Take note of the number of chapters in the books of line you have chosen. The smaller, sweet romances have ten to twelve, with about eighteen pages per chapter. It is important to know what the editor wants because print runs are often set for a particular format. If your manuscript does not fit, it will be rejected.

Each chapter must have action—a conflict, a love scene, or both. It must start with the action and end with a hook. Everything in the chapter moves the story forward. All you need is a few sentences to help you keep the focus, and the story going in the right direction. One page per chapter should be enough to give you a workable outline.

When you have completed the section, go back over your conflicts and resolutions. Make sure you have enough to carry the story and that each reaches a satisfactory conclusion.

Above all, write the story you want to tell.

CHAPTER FOUR

SETTING THE MOOD

There are few things more important in romance writing than setting the mood. Your heroine can be a raven-haired beauty and your hero can ooze virility but, if you place them in a cold and practical environment, you won't have a romance.

The proper setting gives authenticity to the story, creates the emotional tone, and is the background for your characters' actions. As much time should be spent on planning the details that surround your people, as on the people themselves.

How do you choose a setting? Starting with where you live is a good place because, to someone else, it is paradise. You know the sights, sounds, smells and feelings that let you put heart into everything you write. It is comfortable because it is familiar.

Travel experiences can be turned into romance novels. What made you feel romantic? Was it the beautiful hotel where you stayed? The pampering that is part of a wonderful escape? Where did you eat? What did you see that you can use?

Keep notes on the museums you visit and the historical places that are part of a tour. Look at the furnishings, the layout of the rooms, the architecture. Collect pamphlets and brochures, street maps, and restaurant guides.

If you can't go to the place where you want to set your story, the next best thing is a talk with a travel agent. Usually, they are happy to help writers and will give you vast amounts of information. Watch travel films and videos, visit the library, historical society, bookstore, and attend the slide shows that run in community centres. Archives supply access to old diaries and letters that can be invaluable for period writing.

Don't forget to learn about the commercial, professional and industrial enterprises that support the economy of the place you have chosen. Not only does this knowledge increase your understanding of the area, it may give you the answer to what your protagonists are doing there.

You are collecting things that evoke a feeling, the details of how places look, feel, smell. You are creating an environment where the heroine and hero will fall in love.

Does your heroine live in a luxurious apartment in a bustling metropolis or has she settled where she can wander quiet country lanes while daydreaming about the hero? Tell your reader when she watches a sunset or sits by a stream. What is she wearing? What scents fill the air? What textures surround her? Appeal to all of the reader's senses.

Describe the colours, the soft evening breeze, the warm summer sun, the feeling of cold wind against the skin, snow falling from a darkened sky. Let your reader know the name of the perfume the heroine is wearing and the kind of flower the hero has tucked behind her ear. Whether the lovers are on a mountain top or walking in the sand on a Hawaiian beach, your audience wants to share the experience.

Music can play an important part when you are setting the mood. Gentle strains waft from the ballroom. The heroine leans against the balcony and longs for the touch of the hero's lips. He had kissed her the night before when the same song was playing. Now, he is dancing in the arms of another.

Food can also add excitement. The hero dips a sweet, ripe strawberry into castor sugar and gently lays it against the heroine's lips. She takes a bite. A grain of sugar clings to the corner of her mouth and he kisses it away.

Descriptions of foods indigenous to a specific location help create mood and give a sense of authenticity. Learn about exotic dishes and use them. Describe the colours, textures, and flavours. Tell the reader what the table is like. Are the protagonists surrounded with sterling and crystal, or are they in a dimly lit restaurant at the edge of the sea, watching a silver moon hanging in a night-blue sky?

Describing the clothing is another way to bring the reader into a setting. Dress is especially important in historical novels: Victorian hoop skirts, Empire dresses, frills and ruffles and ribbons. Period fashion books, available at the library, will give you the details.

Buy fashion magazines for contemporary romances. The designers show luscious silks to caress the heroine's milky skin, wool to wrap her in luxurious warmth, and cottons to cool her on hot summer nights. But clothing can be used in other ways.

What the heroine is wearing, signals the action in the scene. When she slips into a seductive peach nightdress that caresses every curve, the reader knows a sensual scene is about to take place.

Interweave the clothing with the action: The swirl of a full skirt as the heroine slips through the door in an attempt to escape; the hero's open shirt reveals a bronzed chest, taut with muscle, as he pulls against the rope. The heroine should command most of the reader's attention. A tall, dark-eyed beauty will look stunning in a form-fitting, white silk gown, a single diamond her only jewellery.

A word of caution: don't get carried away. While you are concerned with touching each of the reader's senses, you cannot possibly include all the material you have collected. Everything you use must serve a purpose and be relevant to the scene it is enhancing. If something is sitting there for no reason at all, throw it out, no matter how good it is. Make a note and use it another time.

Setting, either geographical or professional, can provide the reason the lovers meet. It can also introduce conflict between them. They can be co-workers in an office, business adversaries, or on vacation in the same country. Present the places where they are through the protagonists' eyes. Different viewpoints change the perspective. Giving a description of a setting "in viewpoint" is simply avoiding straight narrative detail. The reader is interested in the landscape and the interior decor only as far as it affects the characters. For example, if the hero is waiting for the heroine in her executive office, he would notice the surroundings as part of the story. Perhaps he does not know her well and anticipates her personality from her choice of furnishings.

Try to give all descriptions through the eyes of the character who is thinking or doing something that belongs to the present action. This helps to develop your characters and enhance the background of the plot. Large blocks of description stop the story and make it go flat.

You must fit the setting to the specific needs of the market you have chosen. Contemporary novels require contemporary settings, historical settings should be true to the period, and young adult romance should depict home, school and family vacation spots.

Make the setting an integral part of the plot. If you are in doubt about the importance, ask yourself this question: Why can this romance take place only in this setting? If you don't know the answer then you might have to rethink the scene.

Don't try to pack everything you've researched into one book. There will be others. Keep the action moving and the descriptions part of the excitement. Let the reader see, taste, smell, touch, and hear through the eyes, lips, nose, fingertips, and ears of the protagonists.

Character response to a setting can give insight into what kind of person he/she is. For example, if the heroine is upset because she has been given an average room in an average hotel, instead of the first class accommodation she is accustomed to, it tells the reader she is "spoiled" and has something to learn.

Setting love scenes is important and requires as much attention as you give to the action. Where these scenes take place, helps to intensify the chemistry flowing between the lovers and to arouse a romantic feeling in the reader.

An easy way to do this is to find unconventional settings for tender moments, or to place the protagonists in scenes filled with contrast. For example: The lovers are walking in deep, cold snow. The hero stops suddenly, takes her in his arms and covers her cold skin with hot kisses.

Wind whipping through the trees, warm sun on golden sand, waves breaking against the rocks, are often used as romantic settings because the writer can take them from tranquility to stormy rage. It is from these contradictions of feeling that sexual tension arises. Create romantic settings and you will create sensual love scenes.

CHAPTER FIVE

PLOTTING YOUR ROMANCE

Plotting a romance novel is fun. You have created two attractive people of the opposite sex, placed them in a romantic setting, and now you are going to watch them fall in love.

Think of yourself as all-powerful, with the ability to see the past, present and future. You know everything that has happened, is happening and will happen to your characters so this takes a great deal of mystery out of plotting.

The first thing that occurs, preferably before page five and always in chapter one, is the heroine and hero meet. If your story won't allow for an early physical meeting your hero must be forcefully introduced to the reader who then anticipates his arrival along with the heroine.

Perhaps our heroine has taken a job in a new city and has received a letter from her employer, our hero. The letter is terse, as it outlines her duties, but the handwriting is strong and filled with character. She is understandably apprehensive but, at the same time, filled with anticipation at meeting this rich and powerful man. So is the reader. The protagonists may be physically introduced in chapter two but the hero arrived on the scene in the first few pages of the book.

Establish the sexual chemistry between the protagonists as soon as they meet. There might be distrust, suspicion, denial, or dislike, but they must be curious about, and physically attracted to, each other. The one thing you cannot allow is that they fall into a passionate embrace and escape into the moonlight—or worse, to the bedroom—as soon as they lay eyes on each other. If you do this in the beginning of the book, there is no sustainable tension.

Romance fiction has one central problem . . . the attainment of love. Since this cannot be solved until the last pages of the book, you must give your protagonists difficulties and challenges that stand in their way—complications.

THE COMPLICATIONS are simply the obstacles that you place in the lovers' path to keep them from attaining lasting love. Obviously, the first complication arises when they meet. If you fail to set the conflicts properly, there is nothing to stop them from giving in to the strong attraction between them.

Careful planning is necessary so that when one problem appears to be solved, another arises. Each should be slightly more serious than the last, until one final complication threatens to keep the lovers apart forever. At this point, the heroine, the hero and the reader feel there is no hope.

The type of complication you choose will depend on the story and the line you are writing. The days of having the heroine's difficulties with the hero explained away by declaring he is a male chauvinist, are over. Romances, even young adult series, are dealing with important issues that affect men and women today.

Usually, one or the other is suffering from some trauma. It could be a death, a divorce, even abuse. The internal conflict causes crippling memories of the past, leaving the protagonist wary of falling in love.

External conflicts are also necessary to sustain the plot. These are the obstacles you throw in their way that they cannot control. It could be the arrival of an ex-wife or -husband. It could be work related friction or a professional controversy.

The one thing you are striving for is freshness. There are many romance authors who are turning out new and exciting plotlines. When you are trying to break into the market, you can't afford to submit the same, tired problems.

For each complication tearing your lovers apart, there is the sexual attraction pulling them together. When setting up these push/pull scenes that are the substance of sexual tension, ask yourself: Is this problem really big enough to push them apart? Is this meeting strong enough to pull them together? If not, revise it or take it out.

SEXUAL TENSION is the most important ingredient in your plot, the fuel that drives your story from beginning to end. It is present the moment the lovers meet and continues until that final scene when they promise their eternal, undying love. It is so strong that your reader can feel the desire growing between them.

Perhaps, this is the most difficult part of writing a romance. All the guidelines and how-to books in the world can't teach you how to write sexual tension. When you feel the attraction, your reader will also. Until that time, your rejection letters will contain things like, the conflicts are contrived.

The best place to start is with something you know—true for all fiction. It is easier to put emotion into a scene when you have experienced something similar. Dig into your past, look at the present, search your dreams and draw from them.

Go back to the books you have underlined in coloured pen. Find the sections that are the protagonists' attractions and the parts that are the negative responses. Study these until the strong forces of temptation, and the equally strong forces of resistance, are obvious.

Writing a positive and a negative response in the same sentence or paragraph can result in sexual tension. You have the passionate yearning of the heroine's heart in direct conflict with the cool dictates of her head.

Sexual tension is the unresolved attraction between the protagonists. It is the positive and negative tension that is created when they are in the same room. Attraction pulls them together and conflicts pushed them apart.

The reader begins to ask, "Will they ever be together?" Of course they will. This is a romance. The question is not so much will they get together but how will they get together? The pull of sexual tension is comparatively easy to create. After all, the hero is handsome, virile, and often rich. What woman in her right mind wouldn't be attracted?

The heroine is beautiful, confident, and often successful. She is an exciting challenge to any red-blooded man. All he wants to do, from the moment he lays eyes on her, is sweep her into his arms.

The push is more difficult. It takes planning because the sex drive you've created is not easy to turn off. Pulling the lovers apart should never be contrived. It has to be logical and convincing.

Study the opening conflicts in several books. Pay attention to how the author takes the reader through the logistics of these conflicts and the way background and description is woven into the plot. For example:

Caryn Chapman was aware of Trace the moment he entered the room. It wasn't the absolute strength of the man, although his massive shoulders and six foot, two inch height certainly made that clear. It was the fact that he commanded the attention of everyone around him.

His dark eyes lazily scanned the room, narrowing when they settled on Caryn. At first, she thought he was going to let it go, but when Trace squared those impressive shoulders and permitted the smile to caress the corner of his full mouth, she knew she was lost.

She watched nervously as he made his way through the crowd, stopping to acknowledge the subtle tugs at his sleeve. A smile here, another there—gifts to the women who adored him—only succeeded in increasing Caryn's anxiety.

When one persistent woman detained Trace by demanding his full attention, Caryn broke free from the magnetism that held her. She ran long fingers through the matt of blonde curls, her grey eyes frantically seeking an escape route. Just as she started towards the door at the back of the room, a hand captured her arm to suspend her in time and space.

Caryn felt her breath catch in her throat. She turned and looked up into Trace's disarming smile, his charcoal-black eyes, and she hated herself because she was letting her heart take control of her head . . . again.

In this scene, the hero's height, size and colouring has been established. You also get a glimpse of his personality. That, in the past, something has existed between the two, is obvious. The suggestion that it went unresolved is made through Caryn's desire to get away.

When the heroine "looks up" at the hero, the reader knows she is of moderate height. Her hair and eye colouring are brought in through the action of seeking an escape route. The sexual attraction between the two is evident and the conflict is set up with one word . . . again.

The reader is forced to go on. What are they going to say to each other? How much will be revealed about the past? Were they lovers? Will Caryn accept his advances? And will it lead to rekindled romance?

Of course it will. This is romantic fiction and the resolution is always one of happily ever after. What you have done is pave the way for the central complication in the story that follows.

In YOUNG ADULT FICTION, sexual tension is handled differently. Encounters in these romances are generally innocent—hand holding, breathless sighs, a first kiss. The complication is in the mind of the heroine and usually arises from a problem secondary to the romance.

The protagonists in teen romances are not involved in complex, passionate relationships. They are involved in the problems of growing up. Often, they help each other in the resolution of the secondary conflict. From this they mature and grow closer together. The promise of future love is the core of the plot.

The PLOT CLIMAX is the major turning point that causes the resolution of the story. It is a point of high, dramatic intensity—the complication of all complications.

Throughout the story, you have resolved minor conflicts, and the protagonists have surmounted the obstacles that you've placed before them. Just when everything seems to be working out for the best, the author throws in a heated quarrel evolving out of the most important complication. It is a shocking and unexpected turn of events . . . life's darkest moment. THE DARKEST MOMENT always follows the climax scene and is exactly as the name applies—a moment of great unhappiness for the heroine. The love she longs for is slipping away. She searches for ways to undo what has been done and finds all is hopeless. The scene has reduced the reader to despair.

Now is the time to bring the lovers together. THE RESOLUTION demands your best writing. For two hundred pages, or more, you have kept the reader on edge wondering how the protagonists can possibly solve their terrible problems.

To put your people in a room and let them talk out their difficulties for a page or two, then fall into each other's arms declaring their love, is to cheat your reader.

You do not want a contrived ending any more than you wanted a contrived conflict. The resolution must arise logically in a way that makes the reader feel there is no other way the story can end.

To bring everything to a successful conclusion, it is important to know at the beginning of the novel how it will end. If your story is carefully planned and all the minor conflicts are settled as you go, the one remaining conflict will resolve naturally out of the ones that went before.

Knowing your characters—really knowing your characters—is another way to ensure a satisfactory resolution. By the time you reach the final conflict, and take your heroine through her darkest moment, her personality will make her react in a certain way.

The hero will be predictable, too. You know what he is going to do and how he thinks. You know if his personality will let him go to the heroine or if he has to wait for her to come to him. He will tell you if he needs the assistance of a secondary character to solve his dilemma.

The final exchange between the lovers will be dialogue but something dramatic must bring them to this point. They grow to see their mistakes. Both must admit they are wrong. They have a common problem both wish to solve.

The resolution is the breaking down of the last barrier, bringing the protagonists to the point where they are ready to admit that, without love, there is nothing.

PACING YOUR NOVEL

You have hooked your reader in chapter one, with either brilliant action or a stimulating encounter between the protagonists. You have planned your outline so that the reader is going to anxiously turn the pages at the end of each chapter because you have remembered to include a cliff-hanger, that bit of action, often ending in a question, which forces the reader to go on.

You know the kind of thing: Poor Pauline, tied to the railway tracks by Oil-Can Harry. The train approaches. The whistle sounds. She struggles and cries, "Oh, what shall I do?" and the reader has to turn the page to find out.

You have done all these things and now, you must plan every scene in the novel so that the action in the story is balanced.

The easiest way to approach balance is to keep contrast in mind as you move from scene to scene, from chapter to chapter. For example, an impassioned lover's quarrel might be followed by the heroine's conflicting thoughts about the disagreement. She is angry with the hero's disgraceful behaviour but, at the same time, she is berating herself for overreacting.

These are the quieter scenes that let the reader, along with the character, digest what is happening. They give insight into the protagonists' personality. They are the rest before the next dramatic high point.

The balance you are striving for is the balance between action and information. Too much action and your reader will miss the description and narrative that adds colour to your story and an understanding of the characters. Too little action and the reader will lose interest.

Planning insures good pacing. When you have written your first draft, go over it carefully and count the number of scenes in each chapter. Underline the action scenes in red and the quiet scenes in blue. Then have a look at the balance.

Pacing is subtle but very important. Often it is difficult for the new writer. If you keep contrast always in the forefront when you are planning, you will find you are automatically balancing your scenes.

PLANNING YOUR OUTLINE

The purpose of the outline is to help you transfer that exciting idea into a story with enough substance to carry it for the number of pages you must write. It can't be done in an hour or two. Often, it takes several days, even weeks.

You must live with your idea, think about the plot twists and possibilities, get to know your characters. As elements of the plot come to mind, jot them down on index cards or in a notebook. Keep track of bits of dialogue and action. But, write it down. Don't make the mistake of thinking you'll remember—you won't!

You'll know when you are ready to write the outline. In time, you'll find the way that is the best for you. The following suggestions will get you started.

1. Write in the present tense. Example: Caryn Chapman meets Trace Landon for the first time since he left town four years ago. She is filled with conflicting emotions. Trace is the man she once loved, but he is also the man that cast her aside.

2. Write your outline as if you are telling a story, incorporating details and background into the narrative. Explain who the protagonists are, where and how they meet, the chemistry between them, the major and minor conflicts, and the resolutions. Introduce the minor characters, briefly, as they appear in the story.

Example: Caryn Chapman, 5 foot 4 inches, with short blonde hair and grey eyes, is 24 years old. She lives with her father, Dr. Henry Chapman, and her mother, Nell Chapman, in Sweet River, a small town in Southern Anyplace. Caryn spends most of her time dreaming about racing cars—and Trace Landon. Trace is the driver that left . . . and so on.

3. List all the things that make your novel stand out from the hundreds of others in the book stores. Including this information answers two questions: Is there enough to make an editor want my story? Where am I going to set my scenes?

Write out the major problem that pushes the protagonists apart. Make sure it is appropriate for the line you have chosen. What would be suitable for a contemporary or a young adult novel, is not suitable for a regency romance.

List the secondary problems as they appear in the story. If, while working with the outline or plot, you find these need to be changed, then change them. As you write each twist, ask yourself does it add to, or move, the story. If it does not complicate the primary romantic problem, throw it out.

4. List the important scenes in chronological order. As you work with each crisis, know the darkest moment and the

resolution, and tell where it takes place. Name the characters that appear in each scene, tell how they are involved and what happens to them. Detail the event that brings on the climax—the most intense crisis of the story—then outline the dark moment that follows. There have been minor conflicts and resolutions throughout the story but this is the one that will result in a satisfactory conclusion.

5. You must give as much attention to the final chapter as you did to the first. The hook pulled your reader into the book. You maintained the excitement and suspense throughout the story, and your characters lived. Now, you must end it on a note that will satisfy, and make the reader know it could resolve no other way. You release the sexual tension that has been building since chapter one.

6. Finally, estimate the number of words in the completed novel. Write down the number of chapters and pages. (There is a standard for each category). From this information, you will know approximately how many pages per chapter. For example: You are writing a short, contemporary romance of 50-55,000 words. There are 180-187 pages, and ten chapters, in the books you have read. You know your chapters will be about 18 pages each. The editorial guidelines will help you with this planning.

I cannot stress enough the importance of an outline. As you work through the plot, the theme, conflicts and resolutions, everything will become clear in your mind. When you finally start the novel, it will seem to write itself.

CHAPTER SIX

VIEWPOINT IN ROMANTIC FICTION

In real life, we seldom know what another person thinks until he is ready to tell us. In fiction, we can see into the hearts and minds of others, making the skilful handling of viewpoint a powerful tool.

There is first-person narrative viewpoint, told as if the reader was hearing the story firsthand. This voice makes use of I. Third-person narrative, the preferred viewpoint with many editors, uses she. Then there are multiple viewpoint and omniscient.

Viewpoint (point-of-view, voice) refers to the mind of the character through which the author is telling the story. For example, in the tale of Snow White, the reader identifies with Snow White—the viewpoint character. Ask yourself, "Whose story is this?" and your viewpoint character will be clear.

If the story is written in strictly single viewpoint, then everything that happens is told as that one person sees it, hears it, feels it, or thinks about it. The writer must be consistent. Throwing in something like: Caryn's grey eyes glittered like gems in her striking face, when the author is writing in first-person only, will put the reader off for life.

If you are writing from the heroine's point-of- view, which is probable in romantic fiction, at no time will you present any information that she does not know, has not seen or heard, or that she does not experience herself. Self-descriptions should be kept to what she sees in a mirror, what she is thinking about her appearance, or through conversations with others.

Until recently, single viewpoint has been the technique used in contemporary category romances. Today, even the shorter novels contain brief shifts of viewpoint. Occasionally, authors open their novels with an objective statement of fact about the viewpoint character or the event of the opening scene. This example is from the beginning of Yesterday's Voices.

Jennifer Cantrell stretched her long legs, thankful for the extra room in the plane's First Class section. The flight from New York to Puerto Rico had been a long one, riddled with the delays that seemed to plague all of her Caribbean trips.

She shifted again, her discomfort and impatience, obvious. "I'll be so glad to get home," she muttered, glancing at her gold watch.

"Excuse me?" The soft accent caught her attention.

She had noticed the swarthy Latin man when he'd taken the seat. A flash of perfect white teeth and the jet-black blaze of eyes that instantly put her on the defensive . . . . .

Information is given objectively. The author becomes a reporter, describing places, events and actions. In short category romance, objective narrative is usually used in the beginning of the book, and occasionally at the opening of a chapter, to help set the scene. In the longer historical romances and sagas, however, the author may use such passages at will.

These brief shifts of viewpoint also take place in love scenes. Authors will use the hero's voice to give readers some insight into his feelings and to let them experience his passion.

Shifting to the hero's viewpoint requires skilful transitions. The move is made smoothly and the passage is kept as brief as possible. The writer must never forget that this is the heroine's story.

Multiple viewpoint allows you to enter the thoughts of more than one person although one character still predominates. The minor viewpoint characters exist to highlight the personality of the protagonists and to explain the events in their lives.

The author chooses only the number of characters necessary to make his point. From them, the reader learns what is happening. To make a successful transition there must be a one line break for every change of voice, or a new chapter begun.

Each viewpoint character can only know what he or she has been told or has witnessed. The longer novels, such as historical and super romances, need these characters to tell the story. No one person can see and hear all of the action, or be in all of the places, at once.

These stories open with the spotlight on, or about to be on, the heroine. She might not actually be on stage in the opening scene, but her presence is there through another character. The hero might be reading a letter telling him about her arrival, or he might overhear a conversation about her. Even the thoughts of a minor character can introduce the heroine. The point is, the reader knows it is she who will dominate the story.

If the heroine has been introduced through a minor character, the shift to the major viewpoint should follow quickly. It requires skilled control and technique to make voice changes, from one character to another, within a single scene.

Historical romances are often structured so that the opening scene establishes the background and mood of several members of the family. The focus is then thrown onto the heroine.

For the new writer wanting to use multiple viewpoint in historical or longer contemporary romances, it is advisable to make the shifts from chapter to chapter. Work up to this skill gradually.

Young Adult Romances are written in single viewpoint because it is the best way to establish immediate reader identification. This genre focuses on heroines who are about sixteen years of age. The reader is even younger (12 -15 years) so, for a short time, the girl in the story is the girl they become.

Many of these books are effectively written in first-person narrative, using the pronoun I. This allows the heroine to tell about her problems, thereby bringing the reader directly in touch with her feelings.

Most romance editors look for stories written in third-person narrative. Not only is it the easiest for the author to master, it is the one many readers prefer. Identifying with she is often more comfortable than identifying with I.

The author has numerous latitudes with third-person narrative that may not be present in the other voices. For example: The heroine is standing before her mirror, looks at herself and says: "I have beautiful blonde hair and eyes as green as emeralds. He must think I am attractive." In first-person, she sounds vain.

However, if you take the same scene and shift it to third-person narrative, the heroine would stand before her mirror but the text would read: She stood before the mirror, studying her beautiful blonde hair and emerald green eyes, and wondered if the hero thought she was attractive. Suddenly, the heroine becomes real and the question, feasible.

What you must keep in mind is that your heroine cannot know anything other than her own thoughts, what she is witness to, or what she is told. The only way the heroine can know that the hero was at the theatre last night is if he told her, someone else told her, she was there and saw him, or she went with him. This holds true for first-person narrative, third-person narrative, and multiple viewpoint.

The Omniscient Viewpoint occurs when the author creates a godlike situation. The reader becomes privy to what each character is feeling and thinking. Sometimes the author will go as far as telling the reader there is more to the problem than either of the protagonists realizes.

Seldom can the omniscient be handled with any degree of success. It is rarely, if ever, used in today's romances. Not only does it require a secure grasp of fiction techniques, it removes the reader from the immediacy of the romance. It is difficult to get involved and to "feel" the romance when "god" is telling you about the action!

Viewpoint should be determined when you are drafting the outline. It is wise to include in each scene who the viewpoint character will be. Initially, use third-person narrative, single viewpoint. If shifts are necessary, keep them brief.

Pay attention to voice when you are reading. Study the transitions. Learn why they are necessary and what made them work. When a change of viewpoint is done well, the reader is not aware that it is happening. There is no intrusion.

Once you have written two or three chapters, read carefully to see if the viewpoint character, likely the heroine, is coming through easily. If she seems lifeless or if you are fighting to put words in her mouth, you must take the time to get to know her better.

CHAPTER SEVEN

WRITING SENSUAL SCENES

You cannot write a romance without sensual scenes. The degree depends on the particular line and the type of romance you are writing. Editorial guidelines tell the author exactly what the publishers want, and that ranges from nothing more than hand-holding to hot and steamy sex.

Let's assume you are writing a contemporary novel, leaning towards the sensual line that seems to be the trend today. You have a modern-day hero and heroine with up-to-date sexual attitudes, and guidelines that specify how the scenes should be handled.

There are general principles that are common to all lines.

1. Sexual awareness (tension) should always be present between the protagonists.

2. Sex can be fairly explicit but should not be graphic. It is always in good taste with the focus on the sensuous rather than the sexual. The love bond should be stronger than the physical bond.

3. Sex scenes should never be gratuitously included. They should be part of the plot, fit naturally into the scene, and not be overpowering.

4. The emphasis is on shared feeling and not on male domination.

It is the mutually enjoyed sensual encounters that will give your novel depth and meaning. Love between the protagonists must be genuine if the sex scenes are to be justified and effective.

Sexual attraction is powerful, carrying the lovers away in a flood of desire. But, it is the caring and loving emotions the protagonists share that is the emphasis of the sexual experience. These scenes must be planned in the outline as were the action and conflict. Read, and practise writing isolated scenes. If you are uncomfortable with the level you are writing, the love between the protagonists will be forced and unnatural. Instead of bringing emotion to the reader, they will bring rejection letters from the editor with comments like, the love scenes are contrived.

The following points will help you plan the sex scenes for your novel.

1. Every well-written sex scene has a pattern. At first, as the hero and heroine approach each other, there is a definite physical attraction. This is displayed through actions, thoughts and dialogue. Make use of conversation, even argument, before the physical contact is made.

When one reaches for the other, he or she is either accepted or refused. If the initial response is one of rejection, then the advance must be made again and accepted. The lovers begin to touch and respond to each other's closeness. The fervour increases until it is either consummated in the act of intercourse or there is a break in the passion. If someone withdraws from the embrace, there must be a real and logical reason for them doing so.

2. A new complication arises during or immediately after the love scene to pull the lovers apart, once more. One or the other might feel they have acted impetuously. The heroine is more confused than ever, although the encounter was passionate and sincere. This confusion can be caused by an earlier scene, a misunderstanding, or something in the past that has come back to haunt her.

Perhaps something happened during the embrace that makes the heroine doubt her lover. Did he whisper another woman's name? Was he too aggressive? Did he remind her of someone she'd rather forget? Unless this is the last scene in the book, there can be no peace between them.

At the conclusion of the scene, the thoughts should be the heroine's so that the reader can learn how the encounter has affected her. Unless the scene has moved the plot, there is no reason for it. It will be gratuitous sex.

3. Whatever has taken place in the sex scene is the motivation for the next thing that happens in the plot. The emotions in the scene lead to the confusion, confrontations, complications, or the chaos of the next scene. When you are drafting your outline, lay the groundwork for things to come.

4. Balancing the sex scenes takes skill and experience. How many should you include? How often? How many are too many? How many should be sweet, affectionate encounters and how many should be a consummation of their love?

There are no absolute answers to these questions. Obviously, the "steamier" the line, the more sex scenes you will include. A general rule is that each scene paves the way for a more explicit one to follow. At the end of the book there is the one spectacular scene where both partners are totally satisfied and ready to commit to each other.

Outlining these scenes, with the last triumphant encounter in mind, will help you pace your novel. The importance of good taste can't be overemphasised. Sex scenes included to embellish the manuscript, or those that are borderline pornography, will not sell your novel.

5. The length of the scene will depend on the situation and the action that follows it. It must be long enough to give the reader the satisfaction of a sensual read and must clearly show, through dramatization, how the protagonists feel. Usually, this is a few pages. The one thing you must not do is set a figure in your mind—say four pages—and write that many despite what your characters are telling you. They may want to break apart after two pages or they may be having so

much fun you are going to be hard pressed to separate them after six.

6. The sexual description should be imaginative and poetic. It should never be clinical. Biological terms are used in describing body parts above the waist. (The rise of her firm breasts.) Below the waist, euphemisms are used. (The surge of his manhood.) The use of symbolism is your key to success.

You want to create romantic word pictures for your reader. When you write symbolically, you use objects such as the wind, the ocean, trees and crackling logs to represent the passion. A scene might read as follows:

Jennifer's passion surged to match Enrico's as the frenzied rush of surf washed over them. It seemed as if she was a part of that frenzy; the upheaval that began in some fathomless depth, rising to carry her to its peak. It held her captive, suspended her in time and space, before it released her in an explosion of pleasure such as she'd never known before.

Nature will give you an endless supply of symbols for the creation of love scenes. Look around you. There is much to suggest emotion.

Show the reader the physical and emotional aspects of the heroine's experience. If the hero's hand is stroking her face, she feels his fingers strong against her skin. Emotionally, she is swept to a new level of desire. Rationally, she may be thinking, "I can't do this," but the reader knows she's going to do it anyway.

By making your sex scenes poetic and three dimensional, you keep the reader breathlessly aware of the heroine's total experience.

The level of sexuality, in the remaining categories of romantic fiction, are as follows: In young adult romance there is nothing more than an attraction, some hand-holding, and a few breathless sighs. The story may end in the heroine's first kiss.

Sweet romance takes it one step further. Sexual tension is expressed as an emotional push-pull rather than physical encounters. The heroine's concern is whether the hero really cares about her. She yearns for some sign that he is attracted to her and she hangs on every facial expression, every inflection of voice.

In the sweet romance, reader suspense comes from wondering how the lovers will get together. By comparison, the sensual romances, which include most lines, let the reader enjoy each level of physical contact and the mounting sexual tension between the lovers.

In the erotic historical, the readers are overwhelmed by the hero's endless, and sometimes rough, pursuit of the heroine. Lusty passion, the heroine's intense sexual arousal, mixes with intrigue and views of times past to hold the reader's attention.

These stories end with the hero ready to commit to the often longsuffering heroine. He has mellowed considerably so the reader is secure in the knowledge that the heroine, while leading an exciting life, will be cherished.

Write with your senses. That's the best advice I can give you. Think of colours, of how things look, feel and smell. Fall in love with your heros and live the life you wish for your heroines.

Give as much attention to the setting of the sex scene as you have given to the action and the dialogue. Setting intensifies the chemistry flowing between the lovers. It arouses romantic feelings in the reader. An embrace, as the wind whispers through the palms, and the surf caresses the sand, is far more sensual than an embrace in a doorway.

CHAPTER EIGHT

DIALOGUE

Dialogue is the living, breathing part of any romance novel. When your lovers gaze into each other's eyes and whisper sweet words of passion, the reader sighs with pleasure. When they glare at each other and engage in verbal combat, the reader's heart begins to ache.

Narrative and description set the stage to tell the reader what is going on behind the scenes. Dialogue puts the characters on the stage, alive and visible for the audience.

The main purpose of dialogue is to reveal character, but it is also used to:

1. create sexual tension
2. bring the reader up to date
3. reveal conflict
4. show the protagonists' developing relationship
5. interject humour
6. move the plot forward
7. foreshadow coming events
8. fill in background events
9. show characters' inner feelings

All dialogue must be there for a reason. If you have created something that does not accomplish one of the above, take it out.

The percentage of dialogue to narrative depends on the line you are writing. In young adult romance, for example, about 90 percent of the novel will be dialogue. In the longer lines, such as historicals, the percentage may be fifty or sixty. The average for short, contemporary romance is about 60 percent dialogue to 40 percent narrative. Editorial guidelines should tell you what the publisher wants. Studying the dialogue used in several books will give you an idea of the balance.

Dialogue that opens a novel is called a plunge opening. The reader enters the scene without benefit of narrative explanation so it takes a great deal of skill to write something that won't leave the reader hopelessly confused.

The words must be powerful, involving the reader immediately. They must make it clear who is speaking and lead to the opening action in the story. If you want to use the plunge opening, try writing the first draft, then go back and write the dialogue for page one. You may find it easier because you know your characters, and the logical progression of the action.

YOUR CHARACTERS' VOICE

To be convincing, dialogue must seem to be coming straight from the character's mouth. It takes practice to be able to do this. Writing scenes, independent of narrative or description, is a good exercise. Set up routine exchanges, experiment with emotions, let your people talk to each other without worrying about conflict and resolution.

The first step in writing effective dialogue is developing the ability to "hear" the words. Reading aloud, from some of your favourite novels, may help you. Train yourself to listen to the rhythm of the words. Note the inflections and the phraseology. Find out why you know who is speaking without the author having to make use of speech tags. (Detailed later in this chapter.)

Locate the initial exchange that took place between the hero and heroine. Make a note of that dialogue, along with two or three passages taken at random from the book. Now, compare these with the last conversation the protagonists had together.

There should be a development of feeling and a sense of personal growth. The reader must feel that, finally, the lovers are speaking from their hearts.

When your own story has progressed to the point where the dialogue can be read aloud, do so. It is the best way to test what you have written. If the words don't flow, or you stumble over an expression, then the passage needs to be reworked.

Reading "finished" passages into a tape recorder, or having someone else read them aloud, is another way of assessing the dialogue. When the characters "talk" they should not sound like you. Nor should they sound like every other character. Their voices must be distinct.

The more intimately you know your characters, the easier the dialogue will be. Your outline, showing the complications, and the "interview" giving you insight into the characters' feelings and thoughts, help to determine the words they will say.

Dialogue is a major part of characterization. Your heroine's femininity is revealed in how she feels about herself, her interactions with the hero, and her attitudes towards secondary characters and situations.

The hero is revealed as self-assured, self-centered, gentle or humorous, depending on the words he chooses.

In real life, no two people speak alike so they should not do so in your novel. Even in families, where expressions may be shared and heredity may give a similar tone to the voice, the inflections and speech patterns will vary widely.

When setting your location, pay attention to the development of dialogue. A person from the Mid-west will speak differently than one from the Deep South. The same principle applies to the period of your story. A Regency hero would never tell his lady love that she "looks super in that dress."

Teenagers, in young adult romance, use the current slang and this can be difficult for the author who is not exposed to the age group. You must be familiar with the latest expressions, knowing that they can change before your novel sees print. Play it safe and use only enough of the vernacular to give your story atmosphere.

Profession also has a bearing on the way a person speaks. A doctor's or lawyer's vocabulary will be different from that of a waitress or truck driver. A word of warning: be careful including jargon. Limited use gives tone to your novel. Use too much and you lose the reader.

Good dialogue contains words that match the situation and fit the character's personality, geographical location, and background. It suits the mood of the scene and is consistent with the age and sex of the speaker.

If you do not feel you have accomplished these things, then you have not lived long enough with your character. Go back to the bio and reread it. Ask the interview questions again and see if you can get more in depth answers. You are not programming a puppet, you are creating a living, breathing person.

These rules also apply to the minor characters. Even when they are there simply to contrast the protagonists, they require a personality that shows through in their words.

SEXUAL TENSION THROUGH DIALOGUE

The conversations between the hero and the heroine must either pull them together by bringing out the love they feel for each other, or push them apart through conflict.

The combined push-pull in every scene is accomplished by alternating passages of conflict and misunderstanding with those of passion and adoration. The new writer often finds it difficult to show desire as the protagonists rail against each other.

A most important tool is the speech tag, the "he saids-she saids" that tell the reader who is speaking. A common mistake, made by beginning authors, is trying to use action as a tag word. For example:

"You look happy," Enrico smiled down at her.

There is absolutely no way Enrico could smile down the words. A period needs to replace the comma so that the action is removed from the statement. The sentence would read: "You look happy." Enrico smiled down at her.

Speech tags, such as shouted, exclaimed, and whispered, replace said and do not need to be separated.

"You look happy," Enrico whispered, smiling down at her.

Excessive use of speech tags can annoy the reader and stop the flow of the story. A good rule is: Use them only when they are necessary to show feeling, or to enhance an action.

There is nothing wrong with he/she said. The eye skips over these words while absorbing the identification. The pace is not slowed. Once a speaker has been established, many tag words may be eliminated.

For example: Jennifer has just returned home from an assignment and calls Amy, her editor. The conversation follows.

"Hi! Wondered when you'd get back." Amy's cheery voice greeted her. "I was starting to worry."

Jennifer smiled. There was something so solid about Amy. "Hi, yourself. I got back about an hour ago but you know me . . ."

"Yea. That I do. What came first—the wine or the bath?"

"Both together. In fact, just to show you how important you are, I'm still dripping wet."

"You want to call me later? It's okay, now that I know you're safe."

The reader can tell who is speaking by the way the words are written. If Amy/Jennifer said, had been used in every line, the conversation would not have been as smooth. Obviously, if a third person enters the scene, the writer must identify the speaker.

If you are unsure whether to use tag words, read the passage aloud. Quotation marks help to reduce confusion but, if the section is long, you might find you are losing track of which character is which.

If the dialogue runs on for several paragraphs, uncommon in romantic fiction, repeat the initial quotation marks at the beginning of each new paragraph but do not close them until the speech has ended.

Gestures, facial expressions, and body language work with the dialogue to orchestrate scenes of high sexual tension. The following passage is from Yesterday's Voices. The sentences that illustrate the use of body language are written in boldface type.

Jennifer slipped into the waiting limo, accepted the glass of Pommery, and settled back to enjoy the ride.

"Are you happy?" **Enrico smiled down at her.**

"Yes. The wine is very good."

He shifted slightly so that his free arm rested against the back of the rich leather seat. Over the rim of the fluted crystal he watched her, letting the glass play against his lips.

"I am happy," he said, **his voice stroking her.** "From the first time I saw you, I have dreamed of this moment. The night after the plane, I was awake thinking of what I would do when I found you."

"And what did you decide?"

"This." **His fingers reached out and touched her. They traced the sensuous curve of her neck, threatening to settle on the soft rise of her breast.**

"Don't!" Jennifer gasped and pulled back, her hand flying to cover the bare skin at her neck. Beneath her fingertips was a heartbeat that begged him to come closer.

Although Jennifer tells him to stop, the scene shows a positive reaction to Enrico's advances. Her words reject him while her body accepts them. Dialogue in romance fiction is an indispensable part of the lovemaking. Arms entwine and fingertips brush, while murmurings of love add excitement for the character and the reader.

Conversations grow more intimate as the protagonists get to know each other. Initially, they engage in light banter that can be anything from flirtatious to sexy. Whether they are just breaking the ice or lost in passion, the dialogue should illustrate their relationship, at that point, as completely as possible.

In real life, when we are emotionally stimulated, we tend to speak in condensed, even broken, sentences. Only the speaker with a captive audience, a teacher or minister, for example, expounds at length on any given subject. As a romance writer, you can't afford to do that. One yawn and you've lost your reader forever.

Half-sentences and single words show confusion or interrupted speech. Back to Jennifer and Enrico. She is desperately trying to convince him that they should leave the safety of the committee boat covering the race, and fly to a nearby Caribbean island where a political conflict is taking place. Jennifer wants to scoop the story but Enrico thinks it is too dangerous.

"Jennifer, are you still going on about that? I thought by now St. Georges would have been . . . "

"This is important to me!" She interrupted hotly. "I'm not going to forget it. There's not one good reason why we shouldn't go."

"How about you could get killed? That's a pretty good reason."

"No, it's not. We're not even sure what's happening. So how can you count danger?"

"Jennifer—stop this. You need something else to think about. Come here."

"No . . . "

"Shhh. Come . . . "

"This is insane," she gasped, her eyes fixed on his descending lips.

Try to vary the tempo of the dialogue throughout the novel. Using many speech tags, with verbal directions, slows the action. The pace can be increased by writing several pages of rapid-fire dialogue. The rhythm of the dialogue will establish the momentum of the scene.

Dialogue is an excellent device for incorporating humour into the romance. Not only can light banter be flirtatious and fun to read, it can be an effective vehicle for showing character traits.

Your heroine might resort to humour to cover her true feelings. If she is self-conscious, or perturbed at the hero's remarks, a forced smile and a seemingly lighthearted remark, can add insight into her character.

Even an argument can be written in amusing repartee. Humorous dialogue can also show a loving and intimate relationship. This is particularly appropriate to historical romances in which conversations are less direct and open than in contemporary romances.

Humour, between the protagonists, should never be vulgar or destructive. Nor should it be overused. Don't try to sustain clever repartee beyond its endurance. Treat it like a fine spice, there to add subtle flavour to your story.

As with all dialogue, humour is there for a purpose. Thrown in for no other reason than to amuse, it is not effective. It must move the plot, give information, or set a scene.

The following scene is Enrico's attempt to convince Jennifer that she should take the Caribbean assignment. Still recovering from a failed romance, she is fearful of any time she must share with this powerful man, so she has been reluctant to go. She arrives at the office and is met by Amy, her editor.

Jennifer stopped. "Amy, look at me. What's wrong?"

"This," she said, throwing open the door. "If you call it wrong."

Jennifer stuck her head around the corner and gasped. "What the . . .? What is all this?"

"Flowers. A limo arrived this morning. It took a team of men to pack all this stuff in here. Oh, yeah, one of the guys gave me this." She handed Jennifer the envelope.

There was no mistaking the embossed initials on the flap. "Enrico," she whispered. "I should have known." She took out the note.

Cara Mia: I wanted to fill your room with the scent of the tropics but, for now, this is the best I can do. My promise is to give you all the beautiful flowers of the islands when we are there together. I promise you my everything. E.

"God, Amy," Jennifer moaned, "what am I going to do?"

"Take some antihistamine?" Amy laughed, looking around the blossom-filled room.

The humour in this passage shows Jennifer's hesitation and Enrico's romantic persistence. It also serves to reinforce the closeness between Jennifer and Amy, and adds to Enrico's charm. Obviously, it helped persuade Jennifer to make the trip.

Unless humorous dialogue comes naturally to you, don't write it. Nothing falls flatter than failed humour.

Care must also be taken when writing dialect and accents. Avoid extended use of repeated foreign phrases, words spelled phonetically to reflect regional accents, and extended use of dialect. You want to suggest the exotic, not give your reader a decoding exercise.

Enrico is of Latin decent, a fact that is made clear in the first page of Yesterday's voices. When Jennifer is on the plane, anxious to get home, and mumbles words to that fact, the voice beside her says:

"Excuse me?" The soft, Latin accent caught her attention. The paragraph goes on to describe the swarthy man seated beside her.

Later, Jennifer comments: He uses his lack of English like a shield. It protects him and gives him an advantage I don't know how to fight.

Suggestions of dialect can easily be made by excluding contractions (writing cannot, for can't), and by using a more formal English. Dropping letters, 'Scuse me?, for example, should be used sparingly. In Enrico's case, the use of Cara Mia shows that English is a second language but it does not slow the pace.

Even when Jennifer and Enrico carry on conversations with the Islanders, the suggestion of dialect is made. "Yo, man, you wants a boat?" is much clearer than the more phonetically correct, "Yo, mon, 'yo axed he fo' de boa'?"

If you are using local expressions to illustrate dialect, be sure your reader knows what they mean. If they are not clear in context, they have no place in the story.

The same rules apply for period romances. You can present the era, not only with the characters' vocabulary, but in the tone of the conversation and by what they say to each other. Their behaviour reflects the social customs and attitudes of the day.

YOUNG ADULT romances are dominated by dialogue. The conversations are informal, fast-paced and direct because teenagers have yet to develop subtle social graces.

Bantering is kept to the "in" expressions so you must be careful not to date your writing.

If you don't have young people in the home, listen to conversations on the street, in malls, and on buses. Spend some time with your friends' children. Listen to their music and read the books they are reading.

The demand for young adult books is growing. The time you invest could prove to be very worthwhile.

After the first draft of your novel is written, check your dialogue against the following points.

1. Is the dialogue enhanced by action, reaction, thoughts, and description?

2. Is it brief and fast-paced or are there large passages of narration that break the flow?

3. Was it established where the conversation took place and who was speaking?

4. Does it reflect the temperament, background, and present feelings of the speaker?

5. Is there a good balance between dialogue and narrative? Is there a variation in pace?

6. Is there too much slang? Dialect? Is there enough to illustrate the period or location?

7. Are you writing for the reader or to the reader? Pedantic dialogue has no place in romance novels, unless it is spoken by a secondary character to make a point.

8. Does all the dialogue serve a purpose? Are the exchanges true to life?

9. Is the paragraph construction correct? (Indentation, punctuation and new paragraph for each speaker.)

10. Are the tag words and modifiers used correctly?

11. Is the dialogue romantic? Do the words enrich the sexual tension?

Dialogue is the foundation of the romance. It is through your protagonists' words that their love will "live." It is the means by which you take the reader into another time and share the experience of another place.

Good dialogue will bring tears to the reader's eyes and a flutter to the heart. Give it the time it deserves.

CHAPTER NINE

THE SATISFYING RESOLUTION

In romantic fiction, the end is a reversal of the beginning. The story comes full-circle, returning to whatever critical situation opened the novel. The doubts are balanced with certainty; the people better for their struggle.

How your lovers express their ultimate commitment to each other will depend on the market for which you are writing. The sweet romances end with physical contact that is intensely amorous and full of repressed desire. They usually conclude on the verge of consummation.

Sensual contemporaries often include fully consummated sexual scenes with plenty of erotic description to help the reader share vicariously in the lover's rapture. The key here is to keep the writing tastefully thrilling.

In young adult romances, you not only resolve the conflicts, you highlight the protagonists' character growth. They should gain new insights and maturity. Lingering glances and gentle kisses conclude the scene.

These young lovers are on the threshold of adulthood. They have their entire lives ahead of them so, while the story ends on a "happily-ever-after" note, they are not making a "commitment forever."

No matter what line you are writing, the resolution must be believable. To be believable, it must be planned. You have expended vast amounts of energy getting your lovers in and out of conflicts. You have laughed with them and cried with them, and now, at the end of 300 pages or more, you are tired. You want the whole thing over with, but it's not good enough to simply end it.

Throwing your final scenes together, or tacking on unrelated action simply to resolve a conflict, will likely result in a rejection letter that reads: Your ending is contrived. High impact endings come from high impact resolutions. Too much description and narrative weaken the force; emotional, passionate dialogue strengthens it. To accomplish this, you must know where your story is going before you start to write.

Your outline charted the events that pulled your characters together while pushing them apart. You made sure that the balance of action, dialogue and narrative was effective and that the novel was well-paced. Now, before you start to write the final chapter, go back over that outline and list, in order of occurrence, each problem that kept your lovers apart. Then list all the possible resolutions.

When you begin with the least important complication, and move progressively until you reach the most important, the reader's level of suspense is kept in direct proportion with the intensity of the conflict. The reader will want to stay with you to the end.

Carefully review the scenes of sexual tension. Make sure you haven't constructed impossible barriers for the protagonists to surmount. For example, if you allow your hero to commit an unpardonable act, you have created a character so unsympathetic that no reader will believe the heroine could forgive and forget.

The same thing applies to the heroine. If she is so ill-tempered, so selfish, that she does nothing but nag the hero, no matter how hard he tries to please her, the reader will not buy into the romance.

It is frailty that causes sympathetic characters to falter. Their faults must be those the reader can understand because this is the essence of reader identification and sympathy. Happy endings must be deserved.

While you are analyzing these scenes of sexual tension, make sure you have included plenty of physical contact. Everything from touching to passionate caresses heightens the mutual attraction and makes the reader believe that love will conquer all.

Without a strong, consistent build up of desire, the final submission will seem contrived. The lovers must care deeply for each other, in spite of the problems and differences, to justify a continuing relationship.

Just before the final embrace and the declaration of lasting love, all the problems that have kept the protagonists apart need to be summarized. Often, the most believable endings happen when the author uses dialogue, and the realizations of the viewpoint character(s).

The following, from Yesterday's Voices, illustrates the progression of conflict and resolution.

1. The novel opens on an airplane. Jennifer, returning from an assignment, is seated next to Enrico. Still struggling with the memory of a disastrous love affair, she rejects his offer of friendship. This first conflict is a minor one.

2. The conflict with Enrico appears to be resolved once the trip is over. It resurfaces when Amy, the editor at Holiday Life, chooses him to be Jennifer's photographer for the Caribbean assignment.

3. At first, Jennifer refuses to go but Enrico convinces her that they would be a great team, and that he is no threat. The second complication is resolved.

4. Professional friction and sexual tension increases as the two begin to work together. A more serious conflict erupts when Jennifer hears about a political revolt on St. Georges. She wants to cover the story. Enrico, fearing for her safety, does not. Finally, he gives in and they leave for St. Georges, resolving this conflict.

5. The trip to St. Georges is interrupted by a violent squall, leaving the two shipwrecked on a small, uncharted island. The complication that arises is one of survival. While stranded on the island, Jennifer tells Enrico about her former lover, Alan, and the details of that relationship. They also discuss their dreams and their fears, and the love growing between them. The indecision is resolved when Enrico asks her to marry him and she accepts.

6. The reader feels that all is well. The lovers will be rescued and returned home, to live happily ever after. Unfortunately, when they do get back, Alan is waiting for Jennifer. Jealousy colours Enrico's thinking and the major conflict begins to develop.

7. Amy knows that Jennifer and Enrico belong together. Jennifer agrees to let Amy arrange a meeting with Enrico so that they might talk through their problems.

8. Jennifer is leaving her apartment for Amy's office when Alan arrives. He is arrogant and self-serving, forcing his attentions on her. Meanwhile, Enrico has arrived at Amy's office. When Jennifer fails to appear, he concludes it is her way of saying that she has made her choice.

The crisis seems to resolve when Amy convinces Enrico that something has happened to Jennifer. Amy tells Enrico about the earlier conversation when Jennifer expressed her love for him. Enrico decides to go to Jennifer's apartment and settle it, once and for all.

9. Life's Darkest Moment happens when Enrico arrives at the apartment. The door is ajar and he sees Jennifer in Alan's arms. He presumes her struggling is passion, not her attempt to escape. Enrico confronts them but refuses to listen to Jennifer's explanation.

Before Enrico arrived, the situation with Alan had become increasingly unpleasant. He had forced Jennifer into an embrace and she knew, if she couldn't break free, that he was capable of hurting her.

When Enrico came through the door, Jennifer ran to him, but he pushed her away. Heartbroken, she tries to explain.

"Listen to me! There is nothing with Al. When we were on the island, I told you I loved you and you believed me. Why can't you believe me now?"

"Empty words. Words anyone can say. I have been telling you of my love since the first day we met. My eyes told you every time I looked at you. My lips told you with the taste of my kiss. My body told you each time it was close to yours; each time it felt your sweetness. Everything I am has told you. I do not need to say it with empty words."

"Enrico . . . don't . . . " Jennifer clutched at his arm.

"It is too late, Jennifer. I have tried to give you all of me but you run to your old love. I will try no more."

He threw her hands away from him. "Go. Go to your man. But, know this. You will carry the need for me for the rest of your life."

The heat from his eyes burned into her flesh as he took one long, last look. Then he turned on his heel and stalked out of the room, the steps echoing like gunfire around her.

Jennifer stood, frozen with pain. Never again would she know the treasures of his love. They would be hers only in fantasy—every time she was in another's arms.

And so, LIFE'S DARKEST MOMENT—that time when nothing will ever again be right. Of course, the reader knows it will, but how it will, is a mystery.

10. Jennifer goes to Amy for comfort. She tells Amy how much she loves Enrico, and how hopeless that love is. She also tells her that she's afraid of Alan. After Jennifer leaves, Amy decides to step in. She goes to Alan's apartment and begs him to tell Enrico the truth. When he refuses, Amy says she will initiate an attempted rape charge against him unless he does what he's told. So begins the final resolution.

11. Alan does go to Enrico's home. The scene becomes unpleasant when Alan tells him what really happened. Finally, the two begin to talk. Alan agrees to help Enrico, and the chapter ends with the cliff hanger: "Now, here's what we'll do."

12. Amy sends Jennifer back to St. Thomas on the pretext of covering the maiden voyage of a cruise ship. Since the ship will be in Charlotte Amalie for one day only, the writer must know her way around—that writer has to be Jennifer. She is suspicious but she agrees to go.

13. Once in the tropics, Jennifer is glad she took the assignment. As was prearranged, the tender picks her up the morning after her arrival to take her to the ship. On the way, she tells the seaman: I'm anxious to see this new ship. I hear she's really something. When he replies: You're in for a surprise, that's for sure, the resolution is foreshadowed for the reader.

14. The final resolution takes place on the ship. Enrico is there, and the entire crew is in on the plot. Jennifer, believing she is to have lunch, is in the Captain's cabin. Pretending to be called away, the Captain slips out. Enrico enters. Five pages later, they are promising their undying love. Every conflict has been resolved.

The complications and subplots, that have involved secondary characters, must also be concluded. If the characters have no part in the major resolution between the protagonists, you are free to get rid of them in any way that suits the plot. However, if they meet their end by death, fair means or foul, treat these deaths with sensitivity. Excessive violence has no place in romantic fiction.

I can't stress enough the importance of the ending. Editors are swamped with submissions and often begin by reading the first and last chapters. If the final chapter doesn't meet their standards, they may not read the pages between.

Your ending should be a showcase for your best writing... satisfying, credible, and deliciously romantic. When you have created something you really like, put it away for several days and then make a final check.

* Have you accounted for all the characters?

* Are all the conflicts resolved or are there conflicts and characters that fade away without explanation?

* Is the language poetic, bringing to the reader the beauty of the romance?

* Is there a good balance between the physical and the verbal expression of the lovers?

* Is the ending strong enough to give your reader an emotional experience?

* Is the reader left with the feeling that true love will conquer all?

If you can answer yes to all these questions then you have an ending that is believable and satisfying. Your reader has lived through every heart-wrenching complication you have thrown in the lovers' path and breathlessly shared in every kiss. Your audience deserves the best you can give.

You want to be able to type THE END and know you have created magic.

CHAPTER TEN

PREPARING YOUR SUBMISSION

Presentation plays a large part in the selling of your manuscript. It won't matter that it is the best story ever written if it is filled with misspellings and typing errors. It is unlikely that you will find an editor who will read it.

The first draft was written quickly, the words and thoughts flowing uninterrupted. Editing removed wordiness, contradictions in error, scenes and dialogue that went nowhere, and characters who served no purpose.

The manuscript was edited repeatedly, polished to tighten up sentences and perfect word pictures. You double spaced on good, white bond, left ample margins, made the writing error free, labelled and numbered every page. Finally, it is ready to mail.

Put it away for at least a week. Don't even think about it. Paint the bedroom or weed the garden. Anything. When you have stopped believing you have created a masterpiece, take it out and read it again.

The eye has a terrible habit of reading what you think you have written. When the story is fresh in your mind, you fill in the gaps when an explanation is vague or the heroine acts out of character. Before you submit the manuscript, you must read it as if you did not write it. You must become the audience.

Are there passages that are unclear? Does the reader know why the characters behave as they do? Did everyone stay in character? What about the flow, and the balance of dialogue to narrative? Did the ending cause you to sigh? These question can only be answered if you have let the manuscript "cool."

Very few editors want to see a completed manuscript from a first-time writer. Read the guidelines and follow them. If the editor wants a query letter, or an outline and three chapters, then that's exactly what you send.

The query letter should be no more than two or three pages. It briefly tells the editor what your story is about, who you are, and why you feel the manuscript is for them. Above all, it is perfectly written and presented because you are asking someone to trust your writing skills on the basis of a few words.

An outline is a more detailed description of the novel. You will need five to seven pages for short contemporary, and young adult series. The length of the outline will increase proportionately with the length of the book, to a maximum of twenty-five pages.

Interject description and background as you tell the story. For example:

Lynda Lavine (the heroine) is a twenty-five year old freelance model. Her long black hair, large green eyes, unusually white skin, and tall slim build have kept her in demand for several years. Now, she is faced with making the decision to either undergo surgery to keep up with the industry or to make a career change.

Lynda is not happy with either one. She discusses her options with her best friend, Sally Johnson, thirty-eight years old. She is five feet, six inches tall, with short blonde hair and brown eyes. Sally has been Lynda's agent since she started in the business and the two have formed a strong friendship that extends beyond the professional relationship.

Matt Devine (the hero), six feet, two inches, with dark hair and eyes, a strong muscular build and a dominant personality, has been photographing Lynda for Sunnyday Fashions, one of the country's most prestigious publications. The two have been working closely together for the past four months and have found it difficult.

Lynda is convinced that Matt thinks she is finished as a high-priced model. Nothing could be further from the truth... and so on.

Some authors handle the outline chapter by chapter, including, in narrative form, all the information contained in each. Others tell the story from beginning to end, as the example has illustrated. Either way is acceptable, so use the one you prefer.

Should the editor show interest in your query letter, he will tell you to either send the outline and sample chapters or the completed manuscript. If he has accepted the outline, he will direct you to send the manuscript. Some editors also want the computer disk.

You won't have the time to complete an unwritten novel so my advice is query after you have written the book. Later, when you are famous, you can query an idea.

The manuscript is packed, unbound, in a box or large shipping envelope. The cover page lists your name, address, phone and fax numbers in the upper right-hand corner. In the upper left, is the type of romance you are writing. For example: REGENCY ROMANCE. In the centre is the title and your name as you wish it to appear on the published book. The bottom right-hand corner states the total number of words in the novel.

Word count is accurately determined by computer. If you do not have a computer and are estimating the number of words, count how many are in ten lines. Divide that number by ten to find the average per line and multiply it by the number of lines per page. This tells you the approximate number of words on each page. Now, multiply that by the number of manuscript pages to give the approximate word count.

You may also count the number of words in five pages, divide by five, and multiply that number by the number of manuscript pages. Again, the count is approximate and this must be stated on the cover page.

Word count is extremely important. You will see in the guidelines that each tells you how many words the editor wants. You can't stray far from that number because the print runs are set to accommodate X number of pages. Manuscripts are often rejected because there are too many, or too few, words.

In your submission package is a covering letter that refreshes the editor's memory. Reference him back to any correspondence, tell him briefly what the novel is about, and include an SASE that is big enough to hold the manuscript if he rejects it.

Some authors include only a letter-size envelope and request that the editor let him know the decision and destroy the manuscript if it is rejected. I want my copy back! However, I do include a letter-size, stamped envelope for correspondence and a "submission received" card along with the larger envelope.

The card saves me from wondering if the manuscript got there. It is simply a postcard that says: Your manuscript (the name) arrived in our office (the name and editor) on . . . (a space for the date). I leave a space for any notes the editor wishes to add—like the length of time until I can expect a decision.

Always send the package first-class mail. There is less chance of damage or loss. If the editor has requested the manuscript, write requested material on the envelope to avoid getting buried in the slush pile. Make sure it is addressed to the correct editor!

If you are not certain who that is, phone the main office and ask. Editors change more often than you realise so be sure your editorial information is current.

Once the manuscript is mailed and you have recorded the publishing house, the editor and the date, forget it!

Nothing will send you crazy faster than waiting for the cheque! Start working on another novel.

If the manuscript is rejected, send it right back out to another publisher. After the tenth rejection, it is time to reconsider the book. Take into account all the editorial comment that has accompanied the rejections. If you have nothing but form letters, then it is doubtful you have a saleable manuscript.

A form letter with a handwritten note on the bottom, or a personal letter from the editor, needs your attention. Write and thank him for his time and tell him that you appreciate his direction. If the letter detailed trouble spots, write and tell the editor you are going to correct the errors and resubmit. Then do it as quickly as possible.

Most editors include their stand on simultaneous submissions in their guidelines. If they say no simultaneous submissions then don't send your novel to another publisher while it is under consideration.

Give the editor two to four months to review your work. If you have not heard in a reasonable length of time, write a polite letter requesting status. Give the editor all the information necessary to quickly locate the manuscript. If, after six months, they still have not made a decision then you are free to write and give them a time limit. Once that limit has passed, send the manuscript to another publisher, notifying the original publisher that you have done so.

Delays like this are rare but they can happen. Patience is something every writer learns. If you weigh the number of manuscripts an editor reads every month, besides coping with all the other aspects of his job, you can understand why it takes so long.

Do everything you can to make his job easier. Submit clear, clean copy. Follow the guidelines carefully and include a SASE. Write to thank him for his time if you are rejected. Editors are people—overworked people—and they like to know they are appreciated. The next time you submit, he will remember your work as accurate and your manner as cooperative.

It is up to you to tip the odds in your favour. Do everything you can to sell your work. And don't give up!

CHAPTER ELEVEN

THE MARKETS

The following list does not include all market possibilities but it does give you an overview of the available options. I have omitted the editors' names because of the frequent changes. If you are interested in submitting, write (include a SASE) and ask for the guidelines. The lists include the current editorial staff.

AVALON BOOKS

Division of Thomas Bouregy & Company Inc.

401 Lafayette Street

New York NY

USA 10003

Phone: (212) 598-0222

(800) 223-5251

Fax: (212) 979-1862

LINES PUBLISHED:

Very sweet, well-crafted love stories and career romances containing no explicit sex or graphic violence.

About 50,000 words.

HOW TO SUBMIT:

Submissions are nonreturnable.

Accepts unagented authors, unsolicited manuscripts, outlines and sample chapters.

This is a good starting place for the romance writer.

RESPONSE TIME: Three months.

BANTAM

1540 Broadway

New York, NY

USA 10036

Phone: (212) 354-6500

FAX: (212) 782-9523

LINES PUBLISHED:

Loveswept, six per month

Bantam Women's Fiction, four per month

HOW TO SUBMIT:

Does not publish guidelines. Read the line.

Unagented writers send query.

Agented and published writers, completed manuscript when requested.

Does not accept unsolicited manuscripts, synopses, computer disk submission, dot matrix printing.

RESPONSE TIME: Six to eight weeks.

BERKLEY/JOVE/DIAMOND

200 Madison Ave.

New York, NY

USA 10016

Phone (212) 951-8800

LINES PUBLISHED:

Diamond Wildflower and Homespun, Historicals

One per month in each.

Contemporary mainstream, Romantic Suspense, Regencies

HOW TO SUBMIT:

Guidelines available.

Unagented writers query. Prefers agented writers.

Accepts multiple submissions, queries and synopses. Dot matrix okay if dark and easy to read.

Does not accept unsolicited or computer disk submissions.

RESPONSE TIME: Six to eight weeks

FAWCETT

201 East 50th Street

New York, NY

USA 10022

FAX: (212) 572-4912

LINES PUBLISHED:

Regencies, two per month

Historicals, 2-3 per month, and/or

Contemporaries 2-3 per month

HOW TO SUBMIT:

Guidelines available.

Outline and three sample chapters.

Accepts unsolicited manuscripts, partials, unagented writers and simultaneous submissions.

Does not accept dot matrix or computer disk submissions.

RESPONSE TIME: two to four months.

HARLEQUIN BOOKS

225 Duncan Mill Road

Don Mills, Ontario

Canada M3B 3K9

LINES PUBLISHED:

Temptation, four per month

Superromance, four per month

Privileges, two per month

Regency, two per month

HOW TO SUBMIT:

Guidelines available.

Submission procedures vary from line to line.

Accepts unsolicited manuscripts, partials with synopses, and unagented writers.

Does not accept multiple submissions, dot matrix, computer disk submissions.

RESPONSE TIME: Varies. Usually two months to three months but can be longer.

HARLEQUIN BOOKS

300 E. 42nd Street, 6th Floor

New York, NY

USA 10017

LINES PUBLISHED:

American Romance, four per month.

Intrigue, four per month (Starting a Time Travel sub-series of Intrigue.)

HOW TO SUBMIT:

Guidelines available.

Prefers query: Covering letter with synopsis no longer than five pages. All manuscripts, solicited and unsolicited are read by a freelance reader before they are distributed to staff for final review.

Accepts agented and unagented authors.

Does not accept multiple submissions, dot matrix, computer disk.

RESPONSE TIME: Average time is 12 weeks.

HARLEQUIN PRESENTS AND ROMANCES NOW SUBMITTED TO:

MILLS & BOON LIMITED

Eton House

18-24 Paradise Road

Richmond, Surrey TW9 1SR

ENGLAND

LINES PUBLISHED:

50,000-55,000 words. Sweet, traditional romance. Harlequin Romances, Harlequin Presents

HOW TO SUBMIT:

Guidelines available.

Prefer outline and three chapters but will accept completed manuscript.

Accepts agented and unagented material.

Does not accept multiple submissions, dot matrix, computer disk.

RESPONSE TIME: Usually three months. Mailing increases the time.

LEISURE BOOKS:

276 Fifth Avenue, Room 1008

New York, NY

USA 10001

Phone: (212) 725-8811

Fax: (212) 532-1054

LINES PUBLISHED:

Leisure Books, 11 per month

Lovespell, four per month

HOW TO SUBMIT:

Guidelines are available.

Accepts unsolicited manuscripts, partials with outline and unagented authors.

Does not accept multiple submission, dot matrix, computer disk submissions.

LOOKING FOR TiME TRAVEL, FUTURISTIC and PARANORMAL romances about 90,000 words.

RESPONSE TIME: Two months

NEW AMERICAN LIBRARY

375 Hudson Street

New York, NY

USA 10014

Phone: (212) 366-2504

FAX: (212) 366-2888

LINES PUBLISHED:

Signet Regencies, three every other month

Topaz Historicals, three every other month

Topaz Dreamspun, three every other month

HOW TO SUBMIT:

No specific guidelines.

Prefers query from unagented writers. Prefers agented writers but will look at a strong query.

Accepts multiple submission if you let them know.

Does not accept unsolicited manuscripts, dot matrix, or computer disk submissions.

RESPONSE TIME: six to eight weeks.

PINNACLE BOOKS (Division.of Zebra)

375 Park Avenue South

New York, NY

USA 10016

No phone calls

LINES PUBLISHED:

Mainstream, contemporary romances. Sensual.

No longer than 80,000 words.

HOW TO SUBMIT:

Guidelines available.

Five to seven pages, double spaced narrative plot synopsis with at least one sample chapter including a full sex scene.

Accepts unagented writers.

RESPONSE TIME: At least 12 weeks.

POCKET BOOKS

1230 Avenue of the Americas

Sixth Avenue

New York, NY

USA 10020

Fax: (212) 632-8084

LINES PUBLISHED:

Historical and Contemporary, three romances per month.

HOW TO SUBMIT:

Guidelines available.

Query letter or letter with three sample chapters.

Accepts unsolicited manuscripts, partials with outline, unagented writers, multiple submissions.

Does not accept dot matrix, computer disk submissions.

RESPONSE TIME: Three to four months

ST. MARTIN'S PRESS

175 Fifth Avenue

New York, NY

USA 10010-7848

Phone: (212) 674-5151

Fax: (212) 420-9314

LINES PUBLISHED:

Historical and contemporary romance but not category romance. Want "women in jeopardy", glitz and glamour, mainstream women's fiction.

HOW TO SUBMIT:

No guidelines available.

Synopsis and sample chapter, not complete manuscript.

Accepts unagented writers.

Query for electronic submission.

RESPONSE TIME: Reports "promptly."

SILHOUETTE BOOKS

300 E. 42nd Street, 6th Floor

New York, NY

USA 10018

Phone: (212) 682-6080

LINES PUBLISHED:

Romance, six per month

Desire, six per month

Special Edition, six per month

Intimate Moments, six per month

Shadows, two per month

Harlequin Historical, four per month

HOW TO SUBMIT:

Guidelines available.

Query first with covering letter and two page synopses.

Contacts you in about two weeks if they want to see the manuscript.

Accepts unagented writers.

Does not accept unsolicited manuscripts, multiple submission, computer disk or non-letter quality dot matrix.

RESPONSE TIME: Three months on manuscripts.

STARLOG PRESS

475 Park Avenue South

New York, NY

USA 10016

Phone: (212) 689-2830

Fax: (212) 889-7933

LINES PUBLISHED:

Rhapsody Romance (historical). Bimonthly.

Moonlight Romance (contemporary). Bimonthly.

Futuristic and Time Travel

HOW TO SUBMIT:

Guidelines available.

Send outline and three sample chapters. (Chapters one and two, and the first love scene.)

Accepts unsolicited manuscripts, partials and synopsis, unagented writers, multiple submissions, dot matrix and computer disk submissions.

RESPONSE TIME: 30-60 days.

ZEBRA BOOKS

475 Park Avenue South

New York, NY

USA 10016

Phone: (212) 889-2299

Fax: (212) 779-8073

LINES PUBLISHED:

To Love Again

Couples

Romantic Moments

Short Historicals

Heartfire Historical

Regencies

Multi-cultural

Fantasy Romances

Romantic Suspense

Erotic Thrillers

Kensington Books—Hardcover programme

Z*FAVE, Young Adult and Middle Grade books

Pinnacle (Detailed previously)

With PINNACLE, publishes 35-40 per month

HOW TO SUBMIT:

Guidelines available.

Query letter with 3-5 page synopsis. Editors will request a more in-depth synopsis, chapters or complete manuscript.

Accepts unagented writers.

Does not accept unsolicited manuscripts.

RESPONSE TIME: At least 12 weeks. "Please be patient. We're receiving a great many submissions daily, and sometimes the decision process takes a long time."

Two additional markets should be mentioned.

ATLANTIC DISK PUBLISHERS, INC.

1507 Oakmont Drive, Ste. B

Acworth, GA

USA 30102-1865

Phone: (404) 591-3397

Fax: (404) 591-0369

LINES PUBLISHED:

Established 1993.

Looking at all forms of fiction, including all romance lines.

HOW TO SUBMIT:

Guidelines available.

Completed manuscript on:

Word Perfect 5.0 or 5.1

Microsoft Word for Windows or 5.0

DOS/ASCII

Will accept hard copy if no disk available.

Accepts all fiction except pornography.

All submissions in edited form. Agented and unagented.

Covering letter should include information about yourself and your manuscript.

RESPONSE TIME: 4-6 weeks.

AUDIO ENTERTAINMENT

P.O. Box 461059

Aurora, CO

USA 80046-1059

Phone: (303) 680-6020

Fax: (303) 680-6019

LINES PUBLISHED:

Most genres including historical, contemporary, intrigue, futuristic, paranormal—any good romance.

Publishes two per month.

Increasing product from one-hour stories to 90 min. or three-hour stories.

These are audio romances so writing style must be conducive to being heard.

HOW TO SUBMIT:

Guidelines available.

Ten to twenty page synopsis or 20,000 word novella. Will look at longer novella if plot is highly complex.

If proposal accepted, author will be given option of writing the novella or selling Audio Entertainment the story.
RESPONSE TIME: Six weeks.

To summarize:

1. Write for the guidelines and follow them.

2. Be sure you know the editor's name for the line you are writing. If you don't know, phone the office and ask.

3. Any proposal, query letter, etc. should be error free and properly presented.

4. First-time authors should finish the manuscript before sending out queries. When an editor requests a manuscript, they expect to get it within a week or two. If you cannot produce it, they will question your ability to complete to deadline.

5. Remember, all publishers are looking for new authors. Give them a fresh storyline, present it properly, and show them that you can write—and you will make a sale.

6. All market material is subject to change.

7. If you are interested in publishing young adult romance, read several books that are on the market. When you find the line(s) you are interested in, write that publisher for the guidelines. This field is more specialized than women's fiction.

CHAPTER TWELVE

SUGGESTED PHRASES FOR THE ROMANCE WRITER

This chapter is intended to help you get started. Romantic tension can be a difficult concept for those trying to learn the genre. Often, it is the tag words that makes the difference between acceptance and rejection.

These brief one-liners are so expertly tucked into the dialogue and woven through the narrative that the reader is seldom aware of them. They are the words that let the reader feel the romance.

When I decided I wanted to write romances, I began by reading as many as possible in a short period of time. While I read, I jotted down those expressions that made the scenes come alive for me. I had a notebook for eyes, another for hair, one for movements, one for words of love, and so on. I ended with a pile of books, but I did learn what made tag words effective.

You will develop your own phrases and find unique ways of using tag words. They will help form your style. This list is not intended to be an easy way out, any more than the words and phrases you are collecting should be. If you copy them verbatim, your characters will lack the depth of feeling that only your words can give.

Use this chapter as a way to stimulate your imagination.

FEMALE PHYSICAL CHARACTERISTICS

BODY

her slender white neck

soft, creamy shoulders

exquisitely dainty features

she had an exciting, wild beauty

her body was willowy, slender and reedlike
the milky colour of her skin
her long slender legs led to full, rounded hips
her body was firm, her hips slim
an exciting suggestion of fine hips beneath the dress
her rounded hips and prominent breasts
smooth, silky bosom, fragrant from the touch of the sun
moist satin of her full breasts
breasts strained against the thin fabric of her blouse
ample breasts accented her narrow waist
a wide blue belt at her waist defined the smallness
slim waist flowed into rounded hips and long legs
EYES
eyes that glowed with a savage inner fire
eyes that hid beneath the lushness of her lashes
her eyes shone with serenity
her eyes held an innocence
her grey eyes were filled with life's pain
her extraordinary eyes burned with passion
face full of eyes
eyes closed like fists
a mischievous look danced in her eyes
hatred blazed in her eyes
her eyes gleamed with enjoyment
excitement added shine to her eyes
her eyes moved upwards to his strong chest
her lids slipped down to shade her eyes
she raised her eyes to find him watching her
her eyes darted nervously from one to the other
her eyes grew large and liquid

she gazed at him with dreamy eyes
her eyes widened with alarm
there was false innocence in her eyes
she dropped her eyes before his steady gaze
there was laughter in her eyes
she took a long, admiring look
her eyes were pools of love
there was a steady, impassioned plea in her eyes
her eyes could not hide the things she felt
her eyes drank in his powerful presence
she glanced at his well-defined body
she watched the emotions play across his face
her green eyes lit with laughter
dark grey-green eyes that seemed to fill her face
eyes so blue they reminded him of cornflowers
her luminous brown eyes were fixed on him
bright, clear blue eyes like polished sapphires
the lush, long lashes of her liquid brown eyes
her large brown eyes held hints of gold
hazel eyes that lit with a golden glow
eyeing him up and down, lustfully
her eyes sparkled with the game she was playing
she blinked, feeling strangely lightheaded
shot him a withering glance
her eyes clouded with images of the past
she looked at him hopefully
she found a joyous satisfaction in his gaze
FACE
her face was blushed with eagerness
she felt the colour rise and then subside

exotic cheekbones, out of place in her delicate face

perfect, oval face held wild green eyes

face was arresting and irregular

delicate, patrician features

heart-shaped face, dark and rather delicate

there was both softness and strength in her face

mouth curved temptingly

faintly rosy mouth

moisture resting on her full red mouth

her mouth was a smiling pink rose

the corner of her mouth turned down in sadness

her full lips curved over even white teeth

generous lips parted provocatively

there was a blush of colour on her soft lips

her pretty Grecian nose

HAIR

thick dark hair hung in graceful curves to cloak her shoulders

golden strands softened her face

golden strands that brought spun glass to mind

dark hair tumbled carelessly down her back

a cap of bronze-gold curls

the wind whipped her hair about her face

wisps of hair framed a near-perfect face

tiny strands escaped from the mass of heavy black hair

her hair was a golden mist

her red-gold hair gleamed with the shadows of autumn

light brown curls played around her face

a honey-coloured cap of curls

her hair was dishevelled, reflecting the restlessness of her mood

GENERAL

she was gentle and beautiful—and serenely wise

with movements like a dancer, she approached him

she was a woman of strength but it did not lessen her femininity

moved with a gentle overwhelming grace

she was exquisite, a fragile beauty

in the dim light, she took on an ethereal look

her animated personality was enchanting

carried herself with confidence, unaware of the glances

she was volatile by nature

she had a pampered look about her

FEMALE EXPRESSIONS

BROWS

unconsciously, her brow furrowed

her eyebrows rose in astonishment

her brow was creased with worry

lines of concentration deepened along her brow

she quirked one eyebrow questioningly

her brow was arched and rounded with surprise

there was a fluid line to her brow

perfect brows framed liquid blue eyes

MOUTH

her mouth tightened with determination

her mouth was drawn in anger

her mouth gaped in surprise

her mouth lifting in silent invitation

an icy circle ringed her mouth

a tremor touched the corners of her mouth
her mouth mutely formed the words
SMILES/HUMOUR
resting her chin in her hand, she smiled up at him
he looked at her and the smile faded a little
she met him smile for smile
a thoughtful smile tugged at the corners of her mouth
unaware of how beautiful she was when she smiled
her face lit with an open, friendly smile
it was unthinkable not to return his smile
she smiled but didn't form the words that would have been her answer
it was a smile filled with contentment
she smiled hesitantly
a small smile of enchantment rested on her lips
the slow, secret smile said she understood
her face crinkle into a sudden smile
all she could manage was a trace of a smile
she was eager and alive, and her smile said so
she offered him her smile
she flashed a thankful smile
she grinned mischievously
seeing the expression on his face, she laughed
a flash of humour lit her eyes
her endless gaiety
her amusement quickly died
her lips quivered with the need to smile
there was sheer joy in her laughter
she tried to suppress the giggle but she failed
she murmured, half laughing, half crying

there was a sharp edge to her laughter

the anger vanished when she couldn't keep from laughing

she struggled with a choking laugh

she couldn't keep the laughter from her voice

she threw back her head and let the laughter free

NEGATIVE EXPRESSION

her faint smile was touched with sadness

suddenly, she stopped and forced a smile

she smiled, betraying nothing of her exasperation

she was unable to face his mocking words

she managed a tremulous smile

she was silenced by his dark, angry expression

she saw a frown set into his rugged features

she watched his expression change from desire to distrust

she kept her features deceptively calm

she struggled with the terror of the moment

there was nothing of the joy she felt a moment ago

he seemed to turn on her, to change until she was sure she had never known the real man

there was something distant in the way he looked—and it frightened her

nothing seemed real to her anymore

she was lost in the fear of the moment

FEMALE MOVEMENT

HANDS AND ARMS

her fingers were strong and slim

his skin warmed under her sensitive fingers

she carefully kept her fingers from his

she twined her fingers into his

she felt the wild beat of his heart, pushing against her fingers

she withdrew her hand and quickly turned away

her hand rested on his arm

folding her hands demurely in her lap

restlessly, her hand worried the arm of the chair

she lifted her arms to shield her breasts

stiffly, she clenched her hands and let them hang limply at her sides

she folded her hand over his

her hand smoothed his hair but it was her eyes that loved him

she reached out and touched him, sending electricity racing up her arm

her fists bunched at her sides

she flicked a bit of lint from her dress

she made no attempt to reclaim her hand

she wiped her eyes with the back of her hand

her hand traced the line from his cheek to his jawline

in disgust, she threw up her hands

she quickly uncoupled her hand

she buried her hands in the thickness of his hair

a hand covered her mouth, stifling the cry

HEAD

her answer came when she turned her face away from him

embarrassed, she bent her head to study her hands

she tilted her head, gave him a steady look, and left the room

she gave a tense nod of consent

there was a curt nod of dismissal

she shook her head in dismay
violently, she shook her head
silently, she nodded her consent
she leaned her head back and gazed directly at him
lifting her head, she rested it against his shoulder
she cradled her head in trembling hands
she looked up suspiciously
she shook her head in disapproval
the nod of her head was her only gesture
she tossed her head haughtily
tilting her face upward, she waited for his kiss
she tipped her face to the warming rays of the sun
she nodded woodenly and left the room
she wrinkled her nose before she dissolved into laughter
she raised her chin and refused to look away
SITTING/STANDING
she sank into the chair and laid her head on the desk
wrenching her hand away, she stood up
she forced herself to stand
she leaned back in the chair, her beautiful face turned to the sun
collapsed into the chair as her knees buckled
she rose fluidly from the chair
she fell into bed with a thankful sigh
she settled into the soft, blue cushions
she stood in the doorway, aware of another kind of excitement
she stood motionless in the centre of the room
she woke with a fright and sat upright in the bed
she stood and watched, silently waiting

she stood watching him, wondering if he was ever going
to speak
she sat, carefully watching him as he approached
she sat and tried to be calm but she couldn't forget what
he had said

GENERAL MOVEMENT

she drew back into the room and leaned against the wall
she turned with a start as he touched her arm
she shrugged and managed to say, offhandedly
she turned away, not wanting to hear his answer
she swayed in his arms, not missing a beat of the music
she leaned into the firmness of his body
she leaned lightly into him, tilting her face for his kiss
her steps slowed as the thoughts overcame her
she strolled, nodding at the few people she passed
she moved away, her jaw tightening
she stepped away from the pull of his firm body
she shifted from foot to foot
she took an hurried step toward him
she walked, stiff with dignity
she hurried, not wanting to stop to explain
she withdrew from his arms
she walked grandly out of the room
she stepped out of the circle of his arms
she moved closer to him, waiting for his touch
she moved easily but there was impatience in her step
she hugged her knees to her
she yanked out of his arms
she could feel every muscle tense
somehow, she whirled to face him

she cradled her arms about her

she dug her toes into the sand

she swallowed hard, squared her shoulders, and moved away

she drew her legs beneath her

she watched his broad back as he moved away

she stopped, frozen in time

FEMALE VOICE

she answered quickly, over the thundering of her heart

she spoke eagerly

her voice was shaking and fragile

she murmured quickly

her voice rang with authority

she struggled with her voice as she spoke

she didn't know how sensuous her voice had become

she replied in a weak and faltering whisper

the intensity of her lowered voice

she said, her voice a silky caress

she could barely lift her voice above a whisper

her voice echoed her fatigue

she said firmly

she said in a broken whisper

her voice was calm, her gaze steady

she spoke in a strangled whisper

her reply lacked the ring of authority

she pleaded, her voice faint

she blurted, hardly conscious of her own voice

there was an urgency to her voice

she whispered, her hand at her throat

she was thankful no one noticed the tremor in her voice

she said softly, her eyes narrowing
her voice held a throaty tone
her voice was wonderful, soft and clear
she said in a husky whisper
her voice was deep and dusty
her response was matter-of-fact
her low, silky voice
there was a silver-toned quality to her voice
she lowered her voice, mysteriously
her voice faded
her voice trailed away
her voice rose in defiance
she spoke loudly, the words strange to her
her voice held all the promises of her love
her voice betrayed her
a silken thread of warning in her voice
she said, her voice heavy with sarcasm
her voice cut the silence
she remarked, pleased with her own detachment
her voice cut the silence like a knife
a chilly tone
a tinge of exasperation in her voice
she said, the words choked
there was a bitterness in her tone
her voice hardened
the tone of her voice mirrored her disbelief
she demanded, her voice shrill
she said in a nasty tone
there was an icy edge to her words
she said, glaring at him with cold eyes

she threw at him, her words hot with anger

she said through clenched teeth

her tone was as cold as her stare

she sighed, the words filling her with pain

she had nothing left to give him and she said so

she spat the words like poison from her mouth

the angry words escaped before she could stop them

there was nothing gentle in her tone

MALE CHARACTERISTICS

BODY

he was a tall, black-clad figure

his stance emphasised the strength of his thighs and the slimness of his hips

he was lean, tough and sinewy

the very way he stood told her he had made it

his powerful, well-muscled body moved with panther-like grace

a handsome, compact man who moved with easy grace

he stood in a way that told her he prided himself on his good looks

small-boned and medium height, and walked with a spring in his step

towering over all the other men in the room

his movements were swift and filled with virility

he carried himself with a commanding air

he just stood there, breathing

he was devilishly handsome

she couldn't take her eyes from his long, lean form

tall, beautifully proportioned body

she was acutely conscious of his firm body

the open shirt revealed a mat of crisp brown hair

the unbuttoned neck of his shirt revealed hints of dark, wispy hair

he had a wide-shouldered, rangy body

massive shoulders filled the jacket he wore

broad shoulders carried the burden

his shoulders looked like cast bronze

his shoulders seemed to be a yard wide

powerful set of shoulders

outline of his shoulders strained against his shirt

the muscles rippled under the thin white shirt, quickening her pulse

he was powerful, broad chested and muscular

his hand was rough, giving her a sense of protection

his powerful arms were bare

his arm was bare and silky with hair

his hands were beautiful, long-fingered and strong

his hands were big and square, and used to work

his long, sturdy legs were firmly planted

his legs were bare, browned from the sun

long, sinewy legs

there was such strength in his legs

legs as brown and firm as tree trunks

hard, firm thighs

thighs that rippled with muscle

EYES

eyes that were distant and proud

eyes that glowed with a savage inner fire

his eyes held the glow of purpose

eyes, gleaming black like volcanic rock

the mystery of his eyes beckoned her
eyes that were sharp as they assessed her
eyes like summer lightning
his eyes were dark and insolent
his eyes revealed an independent spirit
eyes were compelling and filled with magic
like magnets, his eyes drew her to him
a faint twinkle touched the depths of his black eyes
his eyes blazed with their passion
clear, observant eyes
snappy eyes looked out from his sun-bronzed face
eyes were hard and passionless
flat, unspeaking eyes prolonged the agony
his burning eyes held her
pale eyes like bits of stone
there was a muted spark of humour in his eyes
a devilish look captured his eyes
the amusement suddenly left his eyes
there was a lethal charm, a calmness in his eyes
raw hurt glittered from the depths of his dark eyes
hatred blazed from his eyes
his eyes filled with contempt
a strange, eager look flashed from his eyes
there was a glint of wonder in his eyes
pain, unspoken and alive, glowed in his eyes
eyes half-filled with promises
a touch of moonlight caught his eyes
his eyes smouldered with the embers of his passion
there was an eagerness in his eyes
the Nordic blue of his eyes

wild, sapphire eyes that filled with desire
hard blue eyes, cold like a glacial lake
blue eyes darker than the darkest sapphires
his grey eyes mimicked silver lightning
grey eyes, so cold they could have been carved from glacial ice
brilliant green of his eyes
warm gold-green eyes were filled with wanting her
eyes the shade of ancient amber
hazel eyes, lit with a golden glow
olive-black eyes, mysterious in their murky depth
the firm set of his jaw, the intensity of his ebony eyes
eyes the colour of coal
eyes darkened with his rage
his blue eyes met hers
his eyes shot up when she spoke
his eyes scanned her face, reading the expression
his eyes clung to hers, struggling with her reaction
his lids swiftly covered his eyes
his appreciative eye scanned her from head to toe
his blue eyes danced, closing the distance between them
his eyes swept over her, unable to hide their approval
his eyes probed the depth of her soul
his dark eyes softened at the sight of her
his eyes were wide with accusation
his eyes blazed with sudden anger
his eyes flashed with outrage
his green eyes bore into her
his cold brown eyes scolded her
his eyes flashed a gentle but firm warning

he watched with an acutely discerning eye
his gaze lowered, following his voice
his eyes were hooded and dangerous, like those of a hawk
his dark, dangerous eyes sought hers
his eyes betrayed his ardor
there was an invitation, deep in his eyes
his eyes seemed to undress her
his eyes darkened with desire
his eyes bathed her in devotion

FACE

there was an inherent strength in a face that was vaguely familiar
pleasure softened his granite-like face
handsome, reserved face
a new contentment lit his face
his features were so perfect they seemed surreal
smooth olive skin covered high cheekbones
face was touched with the beauty of his passion
his profile showed power and endless strength
his profile was honed and self-possessed
clear-cut lines of his profile
a profile outlined against the moonlight
his profile was strong and rigid
rugged and sombre profile
a face bronzed by the wind and the sun
the set of his jaw suggested a stubborn streak
jaw thrust forward
his teeth were white and even, contrasting invitingly with his bronzed skin

his lips parted in a smile that displayed perfect teeth

his mouth was kind and gentle

his mouth was drawn thin with anger

there were lines around his mouth and eyes, but they didn't hide his youthfulness—or his strength

HAIR

manly wisps of dark hair escaped the V of his open shirt

his black hair gleamed with ebony lights

thick, tawny-gold hair

strands of wavy hair threatened his eyes

his hair was black, curly and cut short

thick crop of red hair

light brown hair showed sandy lights

one stray lock fell forward

his hair ruffled in the breeze

unruly dark hair

even sideburns, flecked with grey

light hair was a startling contrast to his tan

hair that was black and silky straight

fine, golden hair of his arms

a dusting of hair across his bare chest

hair that begged for the touch of her hands

his hair was untrimmed like his beard, but there was something about it that suited him

his hair was perfectly groomed, telling her he cared about the impression he made

dark, black hair that invited her touch

he ran a comb through his thick, dark hair

his fingers struggled to tame his thick hair

GENERAL

a massive, self-confident presence
he had an air of authority
his presence was compelling
the strong, clean look of him impressed her
his manner was commanding, making his presence felt
he was devastatingly handsome
there was a restlessness about him
he had a rugged, vital power
he had acquired a polished veneer
his dress was simple and elegant
he held a monopoly on masculinity
the tantalizing scent of his after-shave
the rough look of an unfinished sculpture
a quiet and gentle nature showed through
electricity shot from every pore
he had a magnetism that drew women to him
there was an almost frightening virility
masculinity that sent messages to every woman in the room
colliding with his powerful body
he was deliciously appealing, standing there in the doorway
his dress was plain but rich
arresting good looks that commanded attention

MALE EXPRESSIONS

BROWS

his dark eyebrows arched impishly
he drew his brows together in an agonizing expression
his right eyebrow rose, just a fraction
his eyebrows shot up in surprise

he drew his eyebrows down in a frown
he tilted his brow, his look uncertain
brows drew together in an angry frown
MOUTH
a muscle twitched at the corner of his mouth
thoughtfully, he drew in his lips
a muscle quivered at his jaw
his mouth was a twisted threat
his mouth twisted wryly
his mouth was tight and grim
there was a strange line at the corner of his mouth
a mouth, thinning with displeasure
a mouth, drawn in anger
full, lush promise of his mouth
his clamped mouth and fixed jaw
his mouth opened slightly, a hint of desire showing in his
eyes
SMILES/HUMOUR
the warmth of his smile echoed in his voice
there was a smile in his eyes and it fed a sensuous flame
his smile widened, showing his approval
it was only a courteous smile but it left her weak
he looked away, but the smile remained
he grinned, wiping away all trace of his former animosity
a smile that sent her pulses racing
he eased into a smile
disarmed her with his smile
his face split into a wide grin
he rewarded her with a smile

the slight tug at the corner of his mouth told her he was
going to smile
a smile as sweet as summer rain
his smile was irresistibly devastating
the tight expression relaxed when he smiled
he broke into a lazy smile
a glint of humour finally returned
his mouth twitched with humour
with a ripple of mirth
he turned up his smile
he threw back his head and roared with laughter
when he laughed, the years dropped away
there was a trace of laughter in his voice
he laughed richly
his laughter was wonderfully catching
his laugh was scorn-filled
he stopped, stared at her, then burst out laughing
the teasing laughter filled his eyes
a low, throaty laugh
a deep laugh, rich and warm
with a triumphant laugh, he left the room
the laugh stopped and his eyes began to smoulder
his smile deepened into laughter, rich and full
NEGATIVE EXPRESSION
his mouth became a sour grin
his lips twitched in a cynical smile
a satanic smile spread across thin lips
the smile was as false as his words
he smile blandly, uninterested in her presence
frowned into the glass

suddenly, his face turned grim
he was a glum-faced man
a stern-faced expression
his smile vanished and was quickly replaced by a frown
the brittle smile softened, but only slightly
MALE MOVEMENT
ARMS AND HANDS
he fingered the loose strands of hair, caressing her neck
his fingers cupped her trembling chin
his fingers traced patterns on her cheek
his smooth, cool fingers touched her
he took her arm with gentle authority
he held up a hand, silencing her
his arm firmly about her waist
his hand covered hers possessively
slamming his hand on the desk
he touched her elbow, protectively
he smoothed her hair, pushing strands from her eyes
he held out his hands to her
he slammed one fist against the other
a sweeping motion of his arm
his hand tightened on her arm
his hands locked together behind his head
he touched her cheek, wistfully
he threw up his hands in disgust
he dismissed her with a wave of his hand
he rubbed the back of his hand across his mouth
he shaded his eyes with his arm
HEAD
he shook his head decisively

he nodded grimly
he nodded complacently
he shook his head lazily from side to side
dipping his head slightly, he answered her
he started and lifted his head
with a tip of his head, he motioned for her to join him
it was nothing more than a casual nod from a stranger
he smiled and tipped his head
SITTING/STANDING
he dropped down beside her on the couch
standing, he squared his shoulders and cleared his throat
before he spoke
he sat beside her, stroking the soft hair framing her face
he stood, pushing his hands deep into his pockets
he towered over her, intimidating her
they sat, silently sharing the moment
he rose in one easy motion
he raised himself up on one elbow
wedged into the seat beside her
he sat very still, looking at her intently
GENERAL MOVEMENT
he gave an impatient shrug
he turned on one heel and was gone
roughly, he thrust her away from him
he leaned towards her, his eyes cold and mocking
leaning forward in the chair, he said
he pulled her along behind him
he quickly disappeared into the crowd
he stopped, took a deep breath, then swept her into his
arms

he walked away reluctantly, the slowness of his steps
showing her that he wanted to stay
he paced the room, wearing a path in the thick carpet
his firm body moved beside her
with long, strides, he was beside her
he dragged her back, pulling her hard against him
he was visibly trembling as he came to her
he walked with her, pulling her closely to his side
he moved with an instinctive confidence
lazily, he stretched his legs
he rocked back on his heels
his thigh brushed hers
he grinned and squared his shoulders
he stiffened at her question
MALE VOICE
in a resigned voice
a tone filled with awe, touched with respect
he spoke with staid calmness
his voice was courteous but much too patronizing
his answered in a grudging voice
his tone was apologetic
the huskiness lingered in his voice
he was whistling softly
his hoarse whisper killed the silence
a smooth, insistent voice
the challenge in his husky voice
he asked with deceptive calm
a touch of severity
a voice tainted with mock sincerity
the soft voice urged her on

when he answered her, his voice was warm
his voice was low, with just a hint of a rasp
his voice was a velvet murmur
the rich timbre of his voice
a voice so deep it echoed
voice simmering with passion
mellow voice was edged with control
he fought to control his voice
his voice was heavy with sarcasm
in an exasperated voice he tried to explain
he said, mockingly
there was a cool, disapproving tone to his voice
his voice held a possessive desperation
he warned, seriously
there was an edge to his voice
his tone suddenly became chilly
his voice held an ominous quality
he answered her, his voice dull and troubled
he said tersely
his voice was raw and harsh
there was the cold edge of steel in his voice
the tone was nasty
he insisted impatiently
his voice faded into steely silence
the words cut her heart like the cold edge of a knife
his voice hardened as he spoke the words she didn't
want to hear
there was nothing in his tone to suggest kindness
all the gentle words were forgotten
the words escaping his lips were hard and cruel

he never thought he'd say those words but he had, and it
was too late to take them back

EMOTIONS

HAPPINESS

she felt endless joy and satisfaction

her heart sang with delight

she was blissfully happy

a warm glow flowed through her, bringing her alive

his nearness gave her joy

he looked at her with intense pleasure

he exhaled a long sigh of contentment

he held her, knowing more happiness than ever before

tonight, there were no shadows in his heart

he sang with delight

DETERMINATION

her face was lit with strength

her courage gave her the resolve to continue

she forced herself to move forward

she vowed to show him

she was determined not to see him

he struggled to regain his composure

he showed little sign of relenting

his voice was firm, final

pride kept him from giving in

a sense of conviction that was part of his character

ANNOYANCE

she felt restless and irritable

her response was one of cold sarcasm

she gritted her teeth, her vexation evident

her hands began to shake, increasing her annoyance

she turned away, not waiting for his reply
he gave her a black, layered look
there was a critical tone to his voice
he replied, his voice heavy with irony
he stiffened as though she had struck him
he drawled, a twinge of disapproval in his voice
DEFIANCE
she lifted her chin and met his icy gaze
she swallowed hard, then boldly met his eyes
she abandoned all pretence as she answered him
she stiffened and faced the challenge
every curve of her body expressed her defiance
he plunged on carelessly
he waited, challenging her
he dared her to go through with it
there was defiance in his voice
he pretended not to understand
CONFUSION
she didn't know why she found him disturbing
she hesitated, torn by her emotions
she listened but his words perplexed her
her senses were spinning
she waited, in anticipation and dread
his dark eyes showed tortured disbelief
he sat in dazed exasperation
he stared at her, baffled
a war of emotions raged within him
ANXIETY
she gasped, panic rising within her
hurt and anger clutched at her heart

it gnawed at her confidence
icy fingers twisted around her heart
the tone of his voice chilled her
he fought the disturbing thought
just thinking of it, saddened him
his stomach knotted at the thought of it
the strange surge of affection frightened him
his face darkened with unreadable emotion
RAGE
fury rose to choke her
she gave a hostile glare
she seethed with mounting rage
she was breathless with anger
shock yielded quickly to fury
curses fell from his mouth
he glared at her and stomped away
the restrained anger in his voice
his fiery anger was something she had never seen
his face paled with anger
EMBARRASSMENT
stains of scarlet touched her cheeks
her breath quickened, her face flushed warm
she felt a shudder of humiliation
her blood pounded and her face grew hot
she was helpless at the hands of her embarrassment
he stiffened, momentarily abashed
it was the defeat of humiliation that stopped him
he burned with the painful memory
for the first time, he knew humiliation

he was ashamed because he took advantage of her nature

UNHAPPINESS

wild grief ripped through her

tears rose and she wept, rocking back and forth

her thoughts were jagged and painful

she ached with an inner pain

pain stabbed at her heart

the misery of the night haunted him

he shook his head regretfully

he sat in lonely silence

he didn't notice the pain in his voice

suddenly, all pleasure left him

DESIRE

carried away by her own response, she knew a sense of urgency

she stared longingly at him, knowing she wanted his kiss

her heart leapt in response

she fought the overwhelming desire to be with him

the gaze was a soft caress

his eyes raked boldly over her

his gaze dropped from her eyes to her shoulders to her breasts

he wanted to take her in his arms and let her know what a real man was like

EMBRACING

she buried her face against his throat

she twined her arms about his neck

she settled back, enjoying the feel of him

one step and she was in his arms

softly, his breath brushed her face
he whispered into her hair, drawing her closer
he cradled her in his arms
he pulled her roughly against him
he swept her, weightless, into his arms.
he gathered her in his arms and held her

KISSES
she felt the heady sensation of his lips
her mind relived the velvet touch of his lips
she kissed him, releasing the years of pent up passion
there was an intimacy in the kiss such as she had never known
she felt his lips touch hers, as soft as any whisper
his mouth took hers hungrily
he kissed her with his eyes before taking her with his mouth
his lips brushed against her as he spoke
his slow, drugging kisses
his lips left hers to nibble at her earlobe

LOVEMAKING
she curled into the curve of his body
she was gathered against a warm pulsing body
she caressed the length of his back
she moaned softly as he lay her down
her breast tingled against the coarse hair of his chest
he was running his thumb up and down her palm
his tongue explored the rosy peaks of her breast
his tormented groan was her invitation
his hard body pressed into her
his hands lifted her robe above her hips

These few suggestions should give you an idea of how tag words work. Take the time to make notes when you read. Soon, your own creativity will take over and say, "I can do better than that."

Now, slip into something deliciously soft, wear a sensuous fragrance, put on that piece of music heavy with memory...and start writing the story you want to read.